DreamDinners®

DREAM DINNERS®

Turn Dinnertime into Family Time with
100 Assemble-and-Freeze Meals

Stephanie Allen
and Tina Kuna

WILLIAM MORROW
An Imprint of HarperCollins*Publishers*

HarperCollins books may be purchased for educational, business, or sales promotional use. For information please write: Special Markets Department, HarperCollins Publishers, 10 East 53rd Street, New York, NY 10022.

FIRST EDITION

Library of Congress Cataloging-in-Publication Data

Allen, Stephanie, 1962 Aug. 21–

Dream Dinners® : turn dinnertime into family time with 100 assemble-and-freeze meals / Stephanie Allen and Tina Kuna.

p. cm.

ISBN-13: 978-0-06-078422-5

ISBN-10: 0-06-078422-9

1.Make-ahead cookery. 2. Cookery (Frozen foods). 3. Dinners and dining. I. Kuna, Tina. II. Title.

TX652.A4165 2006

641.6'153—dc22

06 07 08 09 10 ❖/QWF 10 9 8 7 6 5 4 3 2 1

It was a typical November day in the Pacific Northwest: gray, damp, and cozy. My daughter, Karlene, was home for the first time since leaving for college. We drove up to Anacortes, Washington, on Fildalgo Island, the largest of the San Juan Islands, where my parents live. Along the way we picked up my grandma, Karlene's "grammy," my mom's mom. Four generations sitting around the dining room table overlooking the crashing November waves on the beach below my parents' home. My dad built a crackling fire in the fireplace. Our goal: Now that we have given our families the dinners, how do we help them have a successful dinnertime?

With all four generations of dinnertime participants, we came up with some tried-and-true family practices for the successful dinnertime. It was a bittersweet time for our family. Grammy had been diagnosed with terminal cancer and passed away less than a month after this special day. I am so grateful for that day and the wonderful memories we all shared together. This book includes those wonderful memories and more from Tina's family, too.

Dedicated to our families' traditions . . .
and to Grammy.

Contents

Acknowledgments

Thank you to our families for their loving support. Our husbands, children, and parents and our commitment to them are our reason for this book. We can't thank our pioneer franchise owners enough; they believed in our dream and trusted our model, bringing Dream Dinners to their communities. Thank you to our wonderful home office staff, who really make this dream possible with their commitment to serving others, and to our God, who has been opening the door all along this journey.

INTRODUCTION

"What's for Dinner?"

It is perhaps the most common—and for some, nightmare-inducing—question posed in households everywhere seven days a week, 365 days a year. If the sound of those three words sends you reeling, or worse, straight to the nearest fast-food chain or take-out joint, we're willing to bet that two words—Dream Dinners—will change all of that forever. It certainly did for us.

It all started with that timeworn working-mother strategy familiar to the more organized of the species: double or triple a recipe, cook it in one afternoon, then freeze what you don't use for later on in the week. The result is one or two nights off from take-out, frozen pizza, and chicken nuggets. And that was how Stephanie—a working mother of two—achieved her goal of eating dinner with her children every night. But she took the age-old method and gave it a smart twist. Instead of cooking each entree—meat loaf for eight, say—and then freezing it, a method that is efficient but cuts down on taste, she did all of the prep work and then froze the mostly uncooked entrées so they'd be ready to complete later as needed. The result was a freezer full of full-flavored ready-to-cook meals—and liberation from that most dreaded of daily chores: scrambling home after work to pull together a wholesome dinner for the family.

Stephanie's surefire method for always having a good meal on the table had become legendary among her friends, who had been angling (and angling and angling) for years to get in on her "cook and freeze" days. Finally, she gave in to the begging and invited a dozen friends to come into her kitchen with their own pans and dishes and a few bottles of wine. She provided the recipes and enough ingredients for everyone to make twelve freezer-ready dinners, each in proportions to serve six. Soon friends were calling in hopes of making their dinners, too.

Stephanie and Tina had been friends and coworkers for years and were the perfect fit to start this business. Stephanie has a culinary background and Tina a financial and accounting background.

Stephanie and Tina started Dream Dinners because they wanted to make it easier for people to get to the dinner table and enjoy a healthy balance of food and relationships. They wanted to make people's lives easier and encourage them to eat together as a family at least three nights a week.

Dream Dinners is the innovator in the home-meal-solutions industry, originating the concept of hosting small-group assemble-and-freeze meal sessions. The first to introduce this time-saving dinnertime solution nationwide, Dream Dinners invented the concept that offers convenience and a fun interactive environment. Now franchised, Dream Dinners helps busy families in over two hundred stores across our nation save time and money, and makes it easier for them to share healthy, home-cooked meals at the table. Visit www.dreamdinners.com for the location nearest you.

What Are Dream Dinners?

Dream Dinners are healthy, delicious, fuss-free meals made with easy-to-find ingredients that you assemble in multiples and freeze. No more hassles planning and preparing meals, no more hectic postwork, predinner, mid-homework chaos in the kitchen.

A freezer full of meals may be the obvious benefit to preparing food the Dream Dinners way, but there's another—no less important—advantage to having dinner at your fingertips, or at least in the freezer. Dream Dinners encourage families and friends to reconnect around the dinner table. Eating dinner together provides benefits for the whole family, including forming stronger family bonds, sharing important family values, improving communication and problem-solving skills, and saving money.

Indeed, research on the eating habits of families and especially children and teens underscores the impact sitting down together to share a meal can have not only on your family's health but also on their emotional well-being.

Making Mealtimes Matter

Apart from alleviating the stress that comes with racing to get dinner on the table every night, our hope is that the Dream Dinners in this book will make the dinner table much like a round table—for discussion, laughter, debate, and real, uninterrupted conversation. If food is essential for nourishing the body and love is the main ingredient for feeding the soul, where better than the family dinner table to get your fill of both? Throughout the book, you will find Let's Talk, our strategies for making mealtimes the most comfortable time to engage in meaningful conversation. First and foremost, we use tactics other than raising our voices to get everyone to the dinner table. Once everyone is sitting around the table, there are further strategies for encouraging them to engage.

Getting Organized the Dream Dinners Way

The best cooks, whether they are making a single meal or many at one time, have a system or strategy for preparing breakfast, lunch, and dinner that is high on efficiency and low on stress.

Dream "Times Three"

When you assemble a recipe, it is just as easy to make three batches as it is to make one. Assemble the ingredients, step by step, into three containers. Serve one tonight and freeze the others for up to three months.

If you assemble a "times three" dinner twice a week, at the end of the month, you'll have sixteen dinners in the freezer, ready to serve to your family or guests, or to bring to others as house gifts. Cooking "times three" saves time, money, and cleanup!

A few advance tips will make this simple method even easier: first, remember to use larger saucepans and mixing bowls when cooking "times three." This will reduce the number of bowls and pans you have to clean later. Second, invest in good-quality freezer bags, heavy-duty foil, plastic wrap, and perhaps even foil pans. This will keep your regular baking dishes available and eliminate worries about losing your dishes when delivering frozen dinners to new moms or new neighbors. While cooking, make sure you get time-intensive processes started first (for example, browning meat and cooking rice or noodles) and group similar tasks together for efficiency: chopping vegetables, grating cheeses, browning meat, and so on.

How to Avoid Impulse Shopping

Buy only what's on your shopping list, nothing else.

Grocery shop only once each week to save time and money.

Get in and out of the store quickly. We spend an average of forty-seven minutes per trip to the grocery store, according to the market research firm Insight Express. Aim to beat the average.

Visit big box and warehouse stores only once each month. Buying in bulk is great, but most of us can't resist purchasing at least one impulse item on these excursions.

Shop alone. Spouses tend to toss unnecessary items into the cart. Children may plead for junk food incessantly!

Never shop when you are hungry. That cholesterol-loaded, jumbo-size bag of chips is harder to resist when your stomach is growling.

Shopping in advance with a specific shopping list is key if you want to prepare meals in the Dream Dinners fashion. Also make sure to keep your pantry well stocked with staples, including canned goods such as chicken; beef; and vegetable broths; whole and crushed tomatoes; white, black, and kidney beans; favorite oils and vinegars; and herbs and spices, to name a few. And for all of those ingredients that are not in the pantry, create a shopping list.

Begin with the Right Tools, Dishes, and Equipment

We created Dream Dinners with busy cooks in mind. None of the recipes on the following pages requires fancy equipment (where did that special attachment to the stand mixer go?) or special tools for assembly. And while we always aim to freeze as much as we can in space-saving, convenient resealable plastic bags, some dishes require sturdier storage, such as plastic containers. Review each recipe that appeals to you before you determine what kind of baking dishes and mixing bowls will be necessary. When dinners are frozen in these dishes, they all need to be wrapped in plastic wrap and/or heavy-duty aluminum foil. We recommend wrapping them in a layer of both. Skimping on foil can mean the difference between a delicious meal from the freezer and one that tastes subtly of other dishes. Double-bag soups and marinades to prevent accidental spilling as they freeze and thaw. Keep a supply of gallon-size resealable freezer bags at your fingertips and clear space in your freezer, too (twelve family dinners occupy about the same amount of space as a case of soda). If your dishes can't go from the freezer to the oven to the table, here's a tip that is especially useful for casseroles. Line the baking dish with foil, prepare the casserole in it, and freeze. Remove the frozen casserole from the dish in the foil, wrap another layer of foil around it, and return it to the freezer without the dish. When you are ready to thaw and bake it, remove the foil, place it back into the original baking dish, thaw, then bake.

"Research shows that children who eat with their families make healthier food choices than when eating out with their peers."

—Martha Marino, a dietician for the Washington State Dairy Council and a member of the Nutrition Education Network of Washington

Making the Best-Tasting Meals

If you follow a few general preparation and cooking rules, you can successfully prepare every dish in this book—for dinner tonight and for later, too.

- All of the low-fat and nonfat ingredients used in our recipes have been tested and proven not to change the taste of our dinners—only the fat content. If you prefer to use eggs in place of egg substitute, or butter instead of a yogurt-based spread, feel free to do so.
- In all the recipes with cheese, unless a specific cheese type is noted, we use a blend of shredded cheeses to cut the fat content. Combine equal parts of 2 percent Cheddar and Monterey Jack, and low-fat mozzarella. Grate your own or purchase bags of shredded cheeses at the grocery store.
- If not freezing, we prefer fresh minced garlic.
- Unless the herbs are noted as fresh, use dried herbs. They freeze better, impart a more pungent flavor in our recipes, and will hydrate when cooking.
- Yields for fruits and vegetables vary. As a guideline, a small diced or chopped fruit or vegetable equals ¼ cup; a medium one, ½ cup; and a large one, 1 cup.
- Buy the largest cans available at big box stores, to save money and time opening all those small cans. That is why our most frequently used ingredients are listed in cups rather than can size.
- Always preheat an indoor or outdoor grill to high. For meat thicker than 1 inch, grill it at least 5 minutes per side to get that coveted seared outside. To check for doneness, use an instant-read thermometer. If you are holding food to serve 10 to 15 minutes later, or more, cover with foil and expect the internal temperature to rise 5 degrees per 10 minutes as it

rests. If you cook chicken to 150°F and hold it for 10 minutes during guest seating and dinner prayers, it will rise to 160°F and be perfectly tender, while retaining its juiciness.

- Dinners will cook or bake more successfully if they are fully thawed before being put in the oven.

Stumped by what wine to serve? Use our simple and general rules. Seafood loves Chardonnay; red meat and Cabernet are good partners; poultry is pleasing with Zinfandel; pasta with Merlot can't be beat; and most Asian and Mexican dishes taste best with a Chenin Blanc.

Recipe Rescue: When a Dish Doesn't Seem Quite Right

IF THIS HAPPENS . . .	TRY THIS:
Too dry	Add ½ cup chicken stock; cover with foil and steam.
Too soggy	Remove the foil and raise the temperature 50°F.
	Check for doneness every 10 to 15 minutes.
Still frozen	Place the dinner in a glass dish or plastic bag and defrost in the microwave.
Fish tough and chewy	Next time cook over the highest heat your stove offers and cook fast, 5 to 10 minutes per inch of thickness, just until it flakes with a fork. Cook shellfish, such as shrimp and scallops, just until they are opaque.
Cooking time is longer than instructions state	Cooking times vary from oven to oven and can fluctuate based on the temperature of the precooked dish. If any portion of the dinner is not completely thawed, the cooking time will be longer.

What Can You Freeze?

Some foods freeze better than others. Raw meat and poultry, for example, maintain their quality longer than their cooked counterparts because moisture is lost during cooking and even more during freezing. Never freeze food in cans or eggs in their shells. However, once the food is out of the can, you may freeze it.

If you freeze food at a consistent 0°F, it will always be safe to eat, though the quality will suffer with lengthy freezer storage. Each recipe in Dream Dinners gives a suggested freezing limit.

Freshness and Quality

Freshness and quality at the time of freezing affect the condition of frozen foods. If frozen at peak quality, foods emerge tasting better than foods frozen near the end of their useful life. So freeze items you won't use quickly sooner rather than later. Store all foods at 0°F or lower to retain vitamin content, color, flavor, and texture. The freezing process itself does not destroy nutrients. In meat and poultry products, there is little change in nutrient value during freezer storage.

Packaging

Proper packaging helps maintain quality and prevent "freezer burn." It is safe to freeze meat or poultry directly in its supermarket wrapping but this type of wrap is permeable to air. Unless you will be using the food in a month or two, overwrap these packages as you would any food for long-term storage, using airtight heavy-duty foil, (freezer) plastic wrap, or freezer paper, or place the package inside a freezer plastic bag. Use these materials or airtight freezer containers to repackage family packs into smaller amounts. It is not necessary to rinse meat and poultry before freezing. Freeze unopened vacuum packages as is. If you notice that a package has accidentally

Every Sunday night, let your family choose which three dinners to thaw in the refrigerator for the coming week.

Foods That Freeze Best

Uncooked proteins, such as chicken, pork, fish, and beef.

Fresh carrots, zucchini, onions, and celery. Fresh potatoes do not freeze—they turn black. Yuck.

Starch-based dishes dry out more quickly than protein-based entrees when frozen.

Myth: You can't refreeze cooked meat. **Fact:** You can refreeze raw meat if it is in a sauce or marinade. Refreezing meats can cause them to lose moisture and become tough, but when used in a casserole or marinade, meats will cook up with more flavor and will usually be more tender.

Butter and yogurt-based spread will freeze but cream cheese, unless blended with other ingredients, will dry out.

Heavy cream and mayonnaise do not freeze. Substitute cream cheese or sour cream if a recipe calls for mayonnaise as a base for sauces. They both freeze better than mayonnaise.

---

been torn or has opened while food is in the freezer, the food is still safe to use; merely overwrap or rewrap it.

Safe Defrosting

Never defrost foods in a garage, basement, car, dishwasher, or on the kitchen counter, outdoors, or on the porch. These methods can leave your foods unsafe to eat.

There are three safe ways to defrost food: in the refrigerator, in cold water, or in the microwave. It's best to plan ahead for slow, safe thawing in the refrigerator. Small items may defrost overnight; most foods require a day or two.

Cooking Frozen Foods

Raw or cooked meat, poultry, or casseroles can be cooked or reheated from the frozen state. It will take approximately one and a half times longer than the usual cooking time for food that has been thawed.

For faster defrosting, place food in a leak-proof plastic bag and immerse it in cold water. (If the bag leaks, bacteria from the air or surrounding environment could be introduced into the food. And tissues can absorb water like a sponge, resulting in a watery product.) Check the water frequently to be sure it stays cold. Change the water every 30 minutes. After thawing, cook immediately.

When microwave-defrosting food, plan to cook it immediately after thawing because some areas of the food may become warm and begin to cook during microwaving.

Refreezing

Once food is thawed in the refrigerator, it is safe to refreeze it without cooking, although there may be a loss of quality due to the moisture lost through defrosting. After cooking raw foods that were previously frozen, it is safe to freeze the cooked foods. If previously cooked foods are thawed in the refrigerator, you may refreeze the unused portion.

If you purchase previously frozen meat, poultry, or fish at a retail store, you can refreeze if it has been handled properly.

Appetizers

"What can I bring?" It is the question we ask every time we're invited to a dinner party or a special occasion. A quick flip through this chapter will give you more than half a dozen dishes that, when made in batches of three, can be ready for any celebration in a very short amount of time.

If You Like to Entertain . . .

If you like to entertain, but find yourself frazzled before the cocktail party planning begins, consider hosting the Dream Dinners way. Make three batches of Pesto and Red Pepper Torte (page 14), Warm Crab and Artichoke Dip (page 18), and Mu Shu Chicken Wraps (page 22). Pull one of each from the freezer, then pick up cheese, olives, bread, and crackers at the grocery store, and in just a few hours, your guests will be raving about the food and you'll be just as relaxed as they are.

Tri-layered Torte

Make three batches because once guests taste this cheese torte, they'll turn around and invite you to their own party! Once the torte is removed from the springform pan, dust the top with fresh chopped parsley or sprinkle on some chopped walnuts to give it a professional look. Serve with crackers.

Serves 6

For One	For Three	Ingredients
		nonstick cooking spray
8 ounces	1½ pounds	whole salami
3 cups (1½ pounds)	9 cups (4½ pounds)	nonfat cream cheese
1½ cups	4½ cups	yogurt-based spread or butter
2 cups (8 ounces)	6 cups (1½ pounds)	shredded Cheddar cheese
2	6	scallions, chopped
⅓ cup	1 cup	fresh parsley, chopped *or* walnuts, chopped

Spray one (three) 9-inch springform pan(s) with nonstick cooking spray.

Putting the appetizer together

Cut the salami into 1 × 2-inch cubes. In a food processor, with the blade running, grind each cube. Set aside. In the bowl of an electric mixer, cream together one-third of the cream cheese and one-third of the spread with a handheld electric mixer until smooth. Add the ground salami and mix until blended. Spread the mixture into the springform pan, dividing it equally among the three pans if you are preparing a triple batch. Tap the pan(s) on the counter several times to set and even the layer. Cream another third of the cream cheese and one-third of the spread until smooth. Mix in the Cheddar until fully blended. Spread the mixture over the first layer, dividing the mixture equally among the three pans if you are preparing a triple batch. Tap the pan(s) on the counter several times to set and even the layer. Chill the pan(s) in the refrigerator while making the third layer. Cream together the remaining cream cheese and spread with the electric mixer until smooth. Add the scallions and continue mixing until thoroughly incorporated. Spread evenly over the second layer, smoothing with a rubber spatula. Divide the mixture equally among the three pans if you are preparing a triple batch. Tap the pan(s) on the counter several times to set and even the layer.

Scallions are sometimes referred to as green onions. When using scallions or green onions use the dark green parts only.

For an appetizer tonight

Cover with plastic wrap and chill for at least 1 hour or until ready to serve.

Remove the springform ring and use a thin knife to smooth the sides of the torte. Leave the bottom of the pan in place and serve the torte on a platter. Garnish with the parsley or nuts and serve with crackers.

To freeze

Cover with plastic wrap. Label, date, and freeze for up to 2 months. Thaw at room temperature before serving as directed above.

Pesto and Red Pepper Torte

It is so convenient to pull an hors d'oeuvre out of your freezer instead of agonizing over what to take to a party. This dish is exceptionally festive for the holidays when made with red and green layers of pesto. If possible, this recipe should be made a day ahead for the best flavor. Serve with crackers or cut-up vegetables. **Serves 6**

For One	For Three	Ingredients
2 cups	6 cups	butter
2 cups (1 pound)	6 cups (3 pounds)	nonfat cream cheese
¼ cup	¾ cup	store-bought basil pesto sauce
¼ cup	¾ cup	store-bought red pepper or sun-dried tomato pesto sauce
2 tablespoons	¼ cup	chopped fresh parsley
		or
¼ cup (1½ ounces)	¾ cup (4½ ounces)	toasted pine nuts

All of our recipes have been designed using products that are low in fat unless flavors would be compromised. You will see in the ingredients lists which products are best used in each recipe.

Putting the appetizer together

Line one (three) 4-cup bowl(s) with cheesecloth, leaving 4 inches hanging over the edge of the bowl. In a large bowl, cream together the butter and cream cheese with a handheld electric mixer. Spoon ½ cup of the mixture into each bowl. Use a rubber spatula to level and smooth the mixture. Do not stir. Spread 2 tablespoons of the basil pesto evenly over the cream cheese mixture. Spoon ½ cup of the cream cheese mixture over the basil pesto and smooth with the spatula. Do not stir. Spread 2 tablespoons of the red pesto over the cream cheese mixture. Repeat with the remaining cream cheese and pestos, alternating the green and red pestos and ending with the cream cheese mixture. Depending on the size of the bowl, there will be 2 to 4 layers. Bring the edges of the cheesecloth over the top layer and wrap tightly with foil. Refrigerate overnight.

To toast nuts, preheat the oven to 325°F. Spread the nuts on a cookie sheet and bake them just until they start to turn brown, checking the nuts every few minutes. Smaller nuts such as pine nuts will toast more quickly than larger ones such as walnuts.

For an appetizer tomorrow tonight

Peel the cheesecloth away from the top of the bowl and invert the contents onto a serving platter. Remove the cheesecloth. Garnish with the parsley or pine nuts.

To freeze

After freezing overnight, bring the edges of the cheesecloth over the top of the bowl, lift out the torte, and wrap it tightly with aluminum foil. Label, date, and freeze for up to 3 months. Thaw overnight in the refrigerator before serving as directed above.

Baked Clam Dip in a Sourdough Bread Bowl

This showstopper bakes up fresh, warm, and gooey. Serve this dip with fresh cut-up vegetables, cocktail breads, or crackers. **Serves 6**

For One	For Three	Ingredients
1 pound	three 1-pound	round sourdough loaf (loaves)
2 cups (1 pound)	6 cups (3 pounds)	nonfat cream cheese
1 cup	3 cups	nonfat mayonnaise
2 tablespoons	¼ cup plus 2 tablespoons	store-bought horseradish
2	6	6.5-ounce can(s) clams, chopped and drained
4	12	scallions, chopped
		kosher salt
		black pepper

Putting the appetizer together

Trim a 2-inch slice off the top of the loaf (loaves) and reserve. Pull out the inside of the bread, leaving a 1-inch-thick wall. Reserve the inside for dipping or save for another use, such as bread crumbs.

In a large bowl, cream together the cream cheese, mayonnaise, and horseradish with a handheld electric mixer. Add the clams and scallions and mix until incorporated. Season with salt and pepper to taste.

Spoon the mixture into the prepared loaf, dividing the mixture equally among the three loaves if you are preparing a triple batch. Replace the reserved top(s). Wrap the bread tightly in two layers of heavy-duty foil.

For an appetizer tonight

Preheat the oven to 350°F. Place the filled loaf on a baking sheet and bake for 1½ hours or just until the filling bubbles around the rim of the bread top. Serve warm with crackers or the bread pulled from the loaf.

To freeze

Label, date, and freeze for up to 2 months. Thaw overnight in the refrigerator before baking as directed above.

Let's Talk

Does making dinner conversation sometimes feel awkward and uncomfortable? Avoid yes/no questions that can stop a conversation dead in its tracks. Instead, ask open-ended "why," "how," and "what" questions.

Tell me about what happened at . . .

What else can you do with that . . .

How does . . . work

What would you do if . . .

Is there another way to . . .

Warm Crab and Artichoke Dip

Although this dip could be dinner all by itself, it's also a scene-stealer at any cocktail party. The combination of crabmeat and artichokes is so rich, you can use nonfat mayonnaise without missing a bit of flavor. Serve with your favorite breads, crackers, or fresh cut-up vegetables. **Serves 6**

For One	For Three	Ingredients
		nonstick cooking spray
2	6	14-ounce can(s) artichoke hearts, drained and quartered
2 cups	6 cups	nonfat mayonnaise
1 cup (4 ounces)	3 cups (12 ounces)	grated Parmesan cheese
1	3	7-ounce can(s) diced mild green chiles
1	3	2-ounce jar(s) pimentos, drained
3	9	scallions, chopped
1 tablespoon plus 2 teaspoons	¼ cup plus ½ tablespoon	lemon juice
1 tablespoon plus 1 teaspoon	¼ cup	Worcestershire sauce
1 teaspoon	1 tablespoon	celery salt
½ pound	1½ pounds	crabmeat, picked over
1 cup	3 cups	sliced almonds

Spray one (three) 9 × 13-inch baking dish(es) with nonstick cooking spray.

Putting the appetizer together

In a large bowl, combine the artichokes, mayonnaise, Parmesan, chiles, pimentos, scallions, lemon juice, Worcestershire sauce, and salt and stir together until smooth. If the crabmeat is canned or frozen and thawed, squeeze over a colander to remove excess juice. Gently fold the crabmeat into the artichoke mixture. Spread evenly in the bottom of the prepared baking dish, dividing the mixture equally among the three dishes if you are preparing a triple batch. Sprinkle with almonds.

For an appetizer tonight

Preheat the oven to 375°F. Bake, uncovered, for 25 to 30 minutes, until brown and bubbly.

To freeze

Wrap each dish in plastic wrap followed by heavy-duty aluminum foil. Label, date, and freeze for up to 2 months. Thaw overnight in the refrigerator before baking as directed above.

Italian Salsa

Use this version as you would any traditional salsa—as a dip for chips, stirred into cooked rice, or served on top of grilled chicken or fish. If you freeze this salsa, the texture will soften slightly, but it is still delicious. For a sweeter taste, use balsamic vinegar instead of red wine vinegar. Serve with tortilla chips, pita chips, or fresh cut-up vegetables. **Serves 6**

For One	For Three	Ingredients
6	18	plum tomatoes, diced
½	1½	red onion(s), diced
1	3	2.25-ounce can(s) sliced pitted black olives
⅓ cup (1½ ounces)	1 cup (3 ounces)	shredded feta or Parmesan cheese
⅓ cup	1 cup	minced garlic
¼ cup	¾ cup	chopped fresh basil
2 tablespoons	¼ cup plus 2 tablespoons	red wine vinegar
2 tablespoons	¼ cup plus 2 tablespoons	olive oil

Putting the appetizer together

In a large bowl, combine the tomatoes, onion, olives, cheese, garlic, and basil. Add the vinegar and olive oil and mix gently with a wooden spoon. Let stand at room temperature for 30 minutes.

For an appetizer tonight

Spoon one-third of the salsa into a serving bowl and serve.

To freeze

Divide the remaining salsa equally between two resealable freezer bags. Label, date, and freeze for up to 3 months. Thaw before serving as directed above.

Mu Shu Chicken Wraps

Use packaged wonton wrappers and shredded cabbage or store-bought coleslaw mix for these easy-to-make appetizers. You can bake them in your oven or if you prefer them crispy, pan-fry them. **Serves 6**

For One	For Three	Ingredients
		nonstick cooking spray
2 cups	6 cups	diced cooked chicken meat
¼ cup	¾ cup	plum sauce
¼ cup	¾ cup	hoisin sauce
1 tablespoon	3 tablespoons	grated fresh ginger
¼ cup	¾ cup	dry white wine
3	9	scallions, chopped
1	3	12-ounce package(s) shredded cabbage mix
1 teaspoon	1 tablespoon	sugar
10	30	4 × 4-inch wonton wrappers
		olive oil for brushing

Spray one (three) 9 × 13-inch baking dish(es) with nonstick cooking spray.

Putting the appetizer together

In a large bowl, combine the chicken, plum and hoisin sauces, ginger, wine, scallions, cabbage, and sugar and stir together thoroughly. Place approximately ¼ cup of the filling along one edge of a wonton wrapper. Roll the wrapper around the filling, tucking in the ends as you go. Place seam side down in the prepared baking dish(es). Brush the wontons with olive oil.

For an appetizer tonight

Preheat the oven to 350°F. Cover the wraps with aluminum foil and bake for 30 minutes. To pan-fry, spray a nonstick pan with cooking spray and heat over medium-high heat. Add the wraps and cook for 8 to 10 minutes on each side. Add 2 tablespoons water and cover. Cook for 2 to 3 minutes more, until soft.

To freeze

Cover each dish with aluminum foil. Label, date, and freeze for up to 3 months. Thaw before baking as directed above.

How to Be a Dream Hostess

Dream Dinners are designed not only to make midweek meals more relaxing—and delicious—but are also ideal for dinner parties. In fact, the beauty of the dinners is that they can all be made weeks ahead. You can make dessert, too, far in advance of the festivities. For example, make the Tried-and-True Lasagne (page 128) and Pumpkin Icebox Pie (page 232) up to two months in advance. On the day of the party, thaw and bake. Add a loaf of store-bought garlic bread and a tossed green salad and you are the dream host.

Stuffed Braided Bread

This savory treat gets gobbled up every time we make it. For variety, fill the bread with combinations such as Canadian bacon and pineapple, or deli-style roast beef with sliced tomatoes, mozzarella, and basil, or scrambled eggs with ham and cheese. The easiest way to make this bread is to use store-bought frozen bread dough, thawed and raised according to the package directions.

Serves 6

For One	For Three	Ingredients
		nonstick cooking spray
2 pounds	6 pounds	store-bought frozen bread dough, thawed
3 tablespoons	½ cup plus 1 tablespoon	store-bought basil pesto sauce
⅓ cup (2 ounces)	1 cup (6 ounces)	part-skim ricotta cheese
1 cup (6 ounces)	3 cups (1 pound, 2 ounces)	chopped ham
1 cup (6 ounces)	3 cups (1 pound, 2 ounces)	chopped cooked turkey
1	3	4.25-ounce can(s) sliced black olives, drained
1	3	6-ounce jar(s) pimentos
¼ cup	¾ cup	drained and minced sun-dried tomatoes packed in oil
2 cups (8 ounces)	6 cups (1½ pounds)	shredded mozzarella cheese

For One	For Three	Ingredients
¼ cup	¾ cup	nonfat egg substitute
1 teaspoon	1 tablespoon	poppy seeds

Spray one (three) baking sheet(s) with nonstick cooking spray.

Putting the appetizer together

On a lightly floured surface, roll the bread dough into one (three) 18 × 10-inch rectangle(s). Transfer it to the prepared baking sheet(s). Layer the pesto, ricotta, ham, turkey, olives, pimentos, sun-dried tomatoes, and mozzarella lengthwise down the center of the rectangle, dividing the ingredients equally among the three rectangles if you are preparing a triple batch. Cut the dough from the edge to the filling at about 1-inch intervals, creating horizontal strips on either side of the filling. Alternately fold the side strips at an angle and cross them over the filling. Tuck the end pieces under the bread. Brush the top with the egg substitute and sprinkle with poppy seeds. Preheat the oven to 400°F. Meanwhile, cover the stuffed bread with a cloth and set aside in a warm place. Let rise for 15 minutes. Bake for 25 minutes; the top should be golden. Let the bread cool for 10 minutes.

When it comes to entertaining for holidays, there's nothing worth celebrating more than a freezer full of food for guests, especially unexpected ones.

For an appetizer tonight

Slice the loaf into 1½- to 2-inch slices. Serve warm or at room temperature.

To freeze

Remove the bread from the pan when it is cooled completely. Cover with plastic wrap and then a layer of foil. Date, label, and freeze for up to 3 months. Thaw in the refrigerator and warm in a 250°F oven for 20 to 30 minutes, until cheese is melted and golden brown.

Mitchel's Popcorn

Popcorn is an easy treat for everyone, as an appetizer or after dinner when playing a board game with your family. Stephanie's son Mitchel created this savory popcorn, which is transformed by a hit of Tabasco. Popcorn should always be made to order, since it tastes best piping hot. Serve it to take the hunger edge off before dinner on a weeknight or with cocktails before going out to dinner.

Serves 6

For One	For Three	Ingredients
¼ to ½ cup	**¾ to 1½ cups**	**butter flavored vegetable shortening**
1 tablespoon	**3 tablespoons**	**yellow popcorn salt**
1 cup	**3 cups**	**popcorn kernels**
6 dashes	**18 dashes**	**Tabasco sauce**

Putting the appetizer together

Melt the shortening in a large pan or popcorn popper over high heat. Add the salt and popcorn. Add the Tabasco sauce and quickly place the lid on the pan or popper. Cook until the popcorn pops once every 3 seconds. Transfer to a large bowl and serve immediately.

For a snack tonight

Prepare one batch at time, as needed.

Margarita Slush

Keep this in your freezer and you'll be ready for a party any time. The slush must be frozen before serving. **Serves 6**

For One	For Three	Ingredients
¾ cup	**2 cups plus 2 ounces**	**frozen limeade concentrate**
¾ cup	**2 cups plus 2 ounces**	**margarita mix**
One 2-liter bottle	**Three 2-liter bottles**	**club soda**
1½ cups	**4½ cups**	**tequila, optional (substitute equal amount of soda, if desired)**
1	**3**	**lime(s), sliced**

Putting the slush together

Combine 1 (3) cup(s) water with the limeade concentrate, margarita mix, club soda, and tequila or extra soda in one (three) ½-gallon container(s) with a tight lid. Shake to mix well.

For slush tomorrow

Freeze the mixture overnight. Before serving, thaw for 1 hour at room temperature or until the texture is like slush. Pour into a pitcher and garnish with fresh lime slices.

To freeze

Place the sealed plastic containers in the freezer for up to 6 months. Serve as directed above.

Raspberry Margarita Slush

With or without the tequila, this pretty drink is a festive offering for a special summer brunch. To make the nonalcoholic version, replace the tequila with an equal amount of lemon-lime soda. This punch needs to be frozen overnight before serving. **Serves 6**

For One	For Three	Ingredients
1	3	6-ounce can(s) frozen limeade concentrate
1	3	6-ounce can(s) frozen raspberry juice concentrate
1	3	1-liter bottle lemon-lime soda
1½ cups	4½ cups	tequila, optional (substitute equal amount of soda, if desired)
1	3	lime(s), sliced

Putting the slush together

Combine the limeade and raspberry concentrates with 1 (3) cup(s) water, lemon-lime soda, and the tequila or extra soda in one (three) ½-gallon container(s) with a tight lid.

For slush tomorrow

Freeze the mixture overnight. Before serving, thaw for 1 hour at room temperature or until the texture is like slush. Pour into a ½-gallon pitcher and garnish with fresh lime slices.

To freeze

Place the sealed plastic containers in the freezer for up to 6 months. Serve as directed above.

Dinner Parties Made Easy

Create one menu for a season and serve that menu three times during that season. For example:

Pesto and Red Pepper Torte (page 14)

Cremini Mushroom and Caramelized Onion Soup (page 66)

Parmesan Green Beans (page 84)

Wild Rice Salad (page 90)

Provençal Flank Steak (page 140)

Dreamy Peanut Butter and Chocolate Cream Pie (page 234)

Make three of each and you have three dinner parties ready!

Breakfast and Brunch

You know the drill. The alarm goes off, your feet touch the floor, and you're off and running, racing against the clock to get the kids dressed, the lunches packed, the dog walked and fed, yourself pulled together, and last—and sadly often least—breakfast on the table. If weekday mornings have become a scramble of cereal boxes and cartons of milk, gulps of juice and half-eaten toast, or worse—a breakfast bar stuffed in one pocket and a juice box in the other—it's time to fill your freezer with the healthy, home-cooked dishes in this chapter. Prepare them on weekend mornings, when you have a bit more time to spend in the kitchen. Put together Breakfast Burritos (page 40) for Sunday brunch and triple the recipe so you can freeze two batches. During the week, bake one—slide the dish into the oven the minute you wake up and serve it 35 minutes later—after having taken it out to thaw the night before. Bake three batches of Corn Bread Muffins (page 102) instead of one, seal them in a resealable freezer bag and freeze. Pull them from your freezer as needed and reheat them in the oven while you shower and dress. There are plenty of recipes here, from Breakfast Eggs with Potato Crust (page 36) to Breakfast Eggs and Chile Bake (page 42) that can be ready to eat on busy weekday mornings. There are also freezer-friendly offerings for special brunch gatherings and celebrations, such as English Muffin and Ham Strata (page 34) and Huevos Rancheros (page 38) that, when prepared in multiples, will go from oven to table in less than 2 hours.

Classic Breakfast Strata

We lovingly call this our "wedding breakfast," because whenever there is a wedding in our families, we make this up "times three" and feed a crowd before the big event. Because this recipe is made a day ahead and refrigerated overnight, it's perfect for big occasions. **Serves 6**

For One	For Three	Ingredients
		nonstick cooking spray
3 cups	9 cups	nonfat egg substitute
2 cups	6 cups	nonfat milk
1 teaspoon	1 tablespoon	dry mustard
1 teaspoon	1 tablespoon	kosher salt
½ teaspoon	1½ teaspoons	black pepper
1	3	1-pound loaf (loaves) sourdough bread, cut into 2-inch cubes
3 cups (1 pound)	9 cups (3 pounds)	ham, cut into 1-inch cubes
3 cups (12 ounces)	9 cups (2¼ pounds)	grated Cheddar cheese

Spray one (three) 9 × 13-inch baking dish(es) with nonstick cooking spray.

Putting the breakfast together

Combine the egg substitute, milk, dry mustard, salt, and pepper in a large bowl. Set aside.

Line the bottom of the prepared baking dish(es) with enough bread cubes to cover. Follow with 1 cup of the ham and 1 cup of the cheese. Repeat two more times, ending with the cheese. Pour the egg mixture over the strata, dividing the mixture equally if you are preparing a triple batch. Cover with plastic wrap and refrigerate overnight.

For breakfast or brunch tomorrow morning

Preheat the oven to 350°F. Remove the plastic wrap and bake for 1½ hours or until the center is set and the cheese has melted and is bubbly.

To freeze

Cover with plastic wrap and heavy-duty aluminum foil. Label, date, and freeze for up to 3 months. Remove from the freezer 2 days before baking, thaw in the refrigerator, and bake according to the directions above.

If you would like to use the real thing, ¼ cup non-fat liquid egg product is equal to 1 egg. Just crack the eggs and whip until smooth, then use like the liquid product (just remember, there are 5 grams of fat per egg).

English Muffin and Ham Strata

The texture and flavor of English muffins gives this dish a crunchy twist. For the ham, substitute any leftover cooked meat you have on hand, such as chicken. Try jazzing up the recipe with steamed broccoli or asparagus.

Serves 6

For One	For Three	Ingredients
		nonstick cooking spray
6	18	English muffins, cut into small pieces
3 cups (1 pound)	9 cups (3 pounds)	diced ham
2 cups (8 ounces)	6 cups (1½ pounds)	low-fat shredded cheese blend (see below)
1½ cups	4½ cups	nonfat milk
1½ cups	4½ cups	nonfat egg substitute
¼ cup	¾ cup	Dijon mustard
½ teaspoon	1½ teaspoons	kosher salt
½ teaspoon	1½ teaspoons	black pepper

In all of our recipes with cheese, unless we note a specific cheese type, we use a blend of low-fat shredded cheeses, cutting the fat content. Blend equal parts of 2 percent Cheddar and Monterey Jack, and low-fat mozzarella.

Spray one (three) 9 × 13-inch baking dish(es) with nonstick cooking spray.

Putting the breakfast together

Spread the English muffins over the bottom of the prepared baking dish(es) to cover. Sprinkle with half the ham and half the cheese. Repeat to make a second layer, ending with the cheese. In a bowl, whisk together the milk, egg substitute, mustard, kosher salt, and pepper.

For breakfast, brunch, or dinner tomorrow

Pour one-third of the egg and milk mixture over the strata, cover with plastic wrap, and refrigerate overnight. Preheat the oven to 350°F. Remove the plastic wrap and bake for 1½ hours or until the center is set and the cheese is browned and bubbly.

To freeze

Divide the remaining egg and milk mixture equally between two resealable freezer bags. Place one bag in each dish directly on the top layer of cheese. Cover with plastic wrap and aluminum foil. Label, date, and freeze for up to 3 months. Before you bake the strata, transfer it to the refrigerator to thaw for 2 days. Pour the egg mixture over the strata and let it soak overnight in the refrigerator before baking.

Freeze any sauce in a separate resealable freezer bag on top of a casserole so the sauce does not get soggy.

Note: Bake dishes uncovered if you prefer a crispy topping; bake covered if you don't.

Breakfast Eggs with Potato Crust

This is essentially a quiche with a hash-brown crust, perfect for busy weekend mornings. Frozen shredded hash browns work best in this dish. You could use any type of grated cheese, but we like the nutty flavor Swiss cheese imparts.

Serves 6

For One	For Three	Ingredients
		nonstick cooking spray
4 cups (2 pounds)	12 cups (6 pounds)	frozen hash browns
2 cups (1 pound)	6 cups (3 pounds)	nonfat cottage cheese
4 dashes	12 dashes	Tabasco sauce
3	9	scallions, chopped
1 cup (6 ounces)	3 cups (1 pound, 2 ounces)	diced ham
1 teaspoon	1 tablespoon	kosher salt
½ teaspoon	1½ teaspoons	black pepper
½ cup (2 ounces)	1½ cups (6 ounces)	grated Swiss cheese
1½ cups	4½ cups	nonfat egg substitute

Spray one (three) 9-inch deep-dish pie plate(s) with nonstick cooking spray.

Putting the breakfast together

Spread the hash browns evenly on the bottom and up the sides of the pie plate(s) and set aside. In a bowl, mix together the cottage cheese, Tabasco, scallions, ham, salt, and pepper. Spread evenly on top of the hash browns and sprinkle the Swiss cheese on top. Pour the egg substitute over the cheese if you are preparing a triple batch.

For breakfast this morning

Preheat the oven to 350°F. Bake until puffed and golden brown, 30 to 45 minutes.

To freeze

Place one bag of egg substitute on top of each dish and cover with plastic wrap and foil. Label, date, and freeze for up to 3 months. The quiche must be thawed in the refrigerator for 1 to 2 days before baking. Pour the egg mixture over the cheese mixture before baking as directed above.

How to Get Them to the Table

Rather than raising your voice to get everyone to the dinner table, make it fun. For example, play a family theme song that signals what time it is, with the unspoken (or sung) rule that everyone must sit down by the time the song ends. Or give young children a reward for getting to the table first to get things rolling. Perhaps the prize is a special seat or having the chance to pick the menu for the following night. A chart with stars tracking the first one to the table is also effective, especially if the reward is deciding what the next big family outing will be.

Huevos Rancheros

Serve this make-ahead breakfast dish with a dollop of salsa and sour cream or yogurt. You could use precooked sausage links, cut into bite-sized pieces. Green chiles lend a mild, sweet flavor. For a spicy kick, add a few drops of Tabasco sauce to the eggs.

Serves 6

For One	For Three	Ingredients
		nonstick cooking spray
15	45	5-inch corn tortillas
3 cups	9 cups	cooked, crumbled sausage
1	3	7-ounce can(s) diced mild green chiles
3 cups (12 ounces)	9 cups (2¼ pounds)	low-fat shredded cheese blend (see page 34)
2 cups	6 cups	nonfat egg substitute

Spray one (three) 9 × 13-inch baking dish(es) with nonstick cooking spray.

Putting the breakfast together

Arrange 5 corn tortillas in the bottom of the baking dish(es). Layer one-third of the sausage, one-third of the chiles, and one-third of the cheese over the tortillas, dividing the ingredients equally among the three dishes if you are preparing a triple batch. Repeat to make a second and third layer, ending with the cheese. Pour the egg substitute over the top cheese layer, cover with plastic wrap, and refrigerate overnight.

For breakfast tomorrow

When ready to bake, preheat the oven to 375°F. Cover the dish with aluminum foil and bake for about 1½ hours, until the center is set and the cheese is melted and bubbly. Let sit for 10 minutes before serving.

To freeze

If preparing a triple batch, divide the remaining two-thirds of the egg substitute equally between two resealable freezer bags. Place one bag of egg substitute on top of each baking dish and cover with plastic wrap and aluminum foil. Label, date, and freeze for up to 3 months.

The huevos rancheros must be thawed in the refrigerator for 1 to 2 days before baking.

Pour the egg mixture over the cheese mixture before baking as directed above.

Breakfast Burritos

These seasoned scrambled egg- and ham-filled tortillas topped with chile-spiked cream sauce are a great choice for family gatherings. There are two time-saving tricks here: scramble the eggs and cook the bacon before you assemble the burritos and serve them with prepared salsa and sour cream. You can even invite guests to get into the act by making these in assembly-line fashion.

Serves 6

For One	For Three	Ingredients
		nonstick cooking spray
1½ cups	4½ cups	nonfat egg substitute
1 cup (6 ounces)	3 cups (1 pound, 2 ounces)	diced ham
½ cup (5 ounces)	1½ cups (1 pound)	cooked and crumbled bacon
3 cups (12 ounces)	9 cups (2¼ pounds)	low-fat shredded cheese blend (see page 34)
1 cup (8 ounces)	3 cups (1½ pounds)	nonfat cottage cheese
2 dashes	6 dashes	Tabasco sauce
8	24	9-inch flour tortillas
1½ cups	4½ cups	sour cream
1	3	7-ounce can(s) diced mild green chiles
3	9	scallions, chopped

Spray one (three) 9 × 13-inch baking dish(es) with nonstick cooking spray.

Putting the breakfast together

Spray a large skillet and add the egg substitute. Cook over medium-low heat, stirring often to scramble. In a large bowl, combine the scrambled eggs, ham, bacon, 2 cups of the shredded cheese, cottage cheese, and Tabasco and mix together. Fill each tortilla with a rounded ½ cup of the filling. Roll up the tortillas and place 6 of them seam side down in the prepared baking dish(es). In a small bowl, mix together the sour cream and green chiles and spread the mixture over the tortilla rolls, dividing it evenly among the three dishes if you are preparing a triple batch. Sprinkle the remaining cheese and scallions evenly over the top of each dish.

For breakfast this morning

Preheat the oven to 350°F. Cover the dish with aluminum foil and bake for 20 minutes. Remove the foil and bake for 15 minutes more or until the cheese is melted and bubbly.

To freeze

Cover with heavy-duty aluminum foil. Label, date, and freeze for up to 3 months. Thaw in the refrigerator before baking as directed above.

Start children off in the kitchen with easy and safe tasks, such as tearing lettuce for the salad, using a can opener, and toasting bread in the toaster.

Breakfast Eggs and Chile Bake

This brunch dish is ready to serve your overnight guests in the time it takes everyone to make it to the breakfast table. What's more, you get to spend time with your guests, drinking coffee and catching up. Serve this with fresh fruit, coffee, and juice.

Serves 6

For One	For Three	Ingredients
½ cup	1½ cups	low-fat yogurt-based spread or butter, melted
1	3	7-ounce can(s) diced mild green chiles
4 cups (1 pound)	12 cups (3 pounds)	low-fat shredded cheese blend (see page 34)
2 cups	6 cups	nonfat egg substitute
1 teaspoon	1 tablespoon	kosher salt
2 cups	6 cups	nonfat milk
1 cup	3 cups	biscuit mix

Putting the breakfast together

Pour the melted spread into one (three) 9 × 13-inch baking dish(es). Layer the chiles on the bottom of the dish(es). Layer the cheese on top of the chiles. In a separate bowl, combine the egg substitute, salt, milk, and biscuit mix and stir until incorporated. Pour the mixture over the chiles and cheese, dividing the mixture equally among the three dishes if you are preparing a triple batch.

For breakfast today

Preheat the oven to 350°F. Bake for 35 to 45 minutes, until browned and the eggs are set.

To freeze

Cover with a layer of plastic wrap and heavy-duty aluminum foil. Label, date, and freeze for up to 3 months. Thaw in the refrigerator before cooking as directed above.

Karlene's Cottage Cheese Pancakes

Stephanie's daughter, Karlene, created this protein-filled pancake recipe. The batter is so delicious, you'll be tempted to lick it right out of the bowl! Serve the pancakes with maple syrup or a spread and Berry Freezer Jam (page 56).

Serves 6

For One	For Three	Ingredients
		nonstick cooking spray
2 cups	6 cups	pancake mix
1½ cups	4½ cups	club soda
2 tablespoons	6 tablespoons	lemon juice
1 tablespoon	3 tablespoons	baking soda
2 teaspoons	2 tablespoons	ground cinnamon
⅛ teaspoon	½ teaspoon	ground nutmeg
2 cups (1 pound)	6 cups (3 pounds)	nonfat cottage cheese
1 teaspoon	3 teaspoons	vanilla extract
1 teaspoon	3 teaspoons	almond extract

Spray a griddle with nonstick cooking spray.

Putting the breakfast together

In a bowl, whisk together the pancake mix, club soda, and lemon juice. Add the baking soda, cinnamon, nutmeg, cottage cheese, vanilla extract, and almond extract. Stir just until blended.

For breakfast today

Heat a griddle over medium heat to about 375°F. Pour ¼ cup of the mixture onto the griddle for each pancake. Cook the pancakes for 1 minute and 15 seconds per side or until golden brown, turning once. Respray the griddle as necessary.

To freeze

Pour the batter into resealable freezer bags. Label, date, and freeze for up to 3 months. Thaw the batter in the refrigerator before cooking as directed above.

Baked Stuffed French Toast

Pull this out of your freezer when you really want to WOW the people at your breakfast table! Raspberry jam and cream cheese are stuffed into French bread pockets, then topped with an almond streusel crumble. Bake as directed or pan-grill it just like French toast by heating a griddle to medium-high heat, spraying with nonstick cooking spray, and browning each piece of bread for 3 to 5 minutes per side.

Serves 6

For One	For Three	Ingredients
		nonstick cooking spray
8	24	2-inch slices French bread
¼ cup	¾ cup	low-fat yogurt-based spread or butter, softened
¼ cup (2 ounces)	¾ cup (6 ounces)	nonfat cream cheese
½ cup	1½ cups	raspberry jam
1½ cups	4½ cups	nonfat egg substitute
1 cup	3 cups	nonfat milk
½ cup	1½ cups	granulated sugar
½ teaspoon	1½ teaspoons	ground cinnamon
1 cup	3 cups	sliced almonds
¼ cup	¾ cup	dark brown sugar
¼ cup	¾ cup	rolled oats

For One	For Three	Ingredients
2 tablespoons	¼ cup plus 2 tablespoons	all-purpose flour
¼ teaspoon	¾ teaspoon	vanilla extract

Spray one (three) 9 × 13-inch baking dish(es) with nonstick cooking spray.

Putting the breakfast together

Create a pocket in each slice of the bread by cutting a horizontal slit about halfway through each slice. Set aside. In a bowl, combine the spread, cream cheese, and jam and mix together. Spoon 2 tablespoons of the jam mixture onto each slice of bread and lay it in the prepared baking dish(es). Set aside.

In another bowl, combine the egg substitute, milk, granulated sugar, and cinnamon and stir to combine. Pour over the bread, dividing the mixture evenly among the three dishes if you are preparing three batches.

In a bowl, combine the almonds, brown sugar, oats, flour, remaining cinnamon, and vanilla and blend together with your hands until the mixture forms crumbs. Scatter the mixture over the bread, dividing it evenly among the three dishes if you are preparing a triple batch. If you are making breakfast today wait to add the topping until the egg is soaked up.

For breakfast today

Preheat the oven to 325°F. Let the dish sit on the counter for 30 minutes, until one-quarter of the egg mixture has soaked into the bread. Turn over and let the other side of the bread soak for 30 more minutes. Bake, uncovered, for 1 hour or until the egg mixture is no longer liquid and the toast is browned.

To freeze

Cover with heavy-duty aluminum foil. Label, date, and freeze for up to 3 months. Thaw at room temperature before baking as directed above.

Breakfast Apple Bread Pudding

This moist, thick bread pudding will make your home smell like the corner bakery. You can peel the apples or, for a more rustic texture, leave the skins on. To prepare the apples, use an apple slicer, and then cut each slice in half, creating approximately 1 × 2-inch pieces. This dish must be refrigerated overnight before baking.

Serves 6

For One	For Three	Ingredients
		nonstick cooking spray
1	3	1½ pound loaf (loaves) raisin bread, cut into 2-inch cubes
1 cup (4 ounces)	3 cups (12 ounces)	chopped walnuts
2	6	Granny Smith apples, cut into 1 × 2-inch pieces
1 tablespoon	3 tablespoons	lemon juice
½ cup	1½ cups	low-fat yogurt-based spread or butter, melted
½ cup	1½ cups	granulated sugar
1 tablespoon	3 tablespoons	ground cinnamon
1¼ cups	3¾ cups	nonfat egg substitute
1 cup	3 cups	brown sugar
1¼ cups	3¾ cups	nonfat half-and-half

For One	For Three	Ingredients
1¼ cups	**3¾ cups**	**nonfat milk**
1 teaspoon	**1 tablespoon**	**vanilla extract**

Spray one (three) 9 × 13-inch baking dish(es) with nonstick cooking spray.

Putting the breakfast together

In a large bowl, combine the bread and walnuts. Spread the mixture on the bottom of the prepared baking dish(es), dividing it equally if you are preparing a triple batch. In a large bowl, combine the apples and lemon juice and toss to coat. Add the melted spread, sugar, and half of the cinnamon. Gently toss with the bread and walnuts in the baking dish(es), dividing the mixture equally among the three dishes if you are preparing a triple batch. In a separate bowl, mix together the egg substitute, brown sugar, half-and-half, milk, vanilla, and remaining cinnamon.

For breakfast tomorrow morning

Pour the egg mixture over the bread mixture, using only one-third of it if you have prepared a triple batch. Cover with aluminum foil and refrigerate overnight. Set the remaining egg mixture aside. In the morning, preheat the oven to 375°F. Bake for 1½ hours or until set and the top is puffy and browned. Let sit for 10 minutes before serving.

To freeze

Divide the remaining egg mixture equally between two resealable freezer bags. Place one bag on top of each baking dish and cover with plastic wrap and foil. Label, date, and freeze for up to 3 months. The bread pudding must be thawed in the refrigerator for 1 to 2 days before baking. To bake, pour the egg mixture evenly over the bread mixture in the pan and bake as directed above.

Zucchini-Cranberry Bread or Muffins

The combination of green zucchini and red cranberries makes this the perfect holiday bread. This batter can also be poured into lined muffin tins and frozen.

Serves 6 to 10

For One	For Three	Ingredients
		nonstick cooking spray
2 teaspoons	6 teaspoons	granulated sugar
2½ cups	7½ cups	all-purpose flour
2 teaspoons	6 teaspoons	baking powder
¼ teaspoon	¾ teaspoon	kosher salt
1½ cups	4½ cups	confectioners' sugar
1 cup	3 cups	low-fat yogurt-based spread or butter
1 cup	3 cups	nonfat egg substitute
¼ teaspoon	¾ teaspoon	almond extract
½ teaspoon	1½ teaspoons	vanilla extract
zest of 1	zest of 3	orange(s), grated
2 cups	6 cups	zucchini, grated
1 cup	3 cups	fresh or frozen cranberries

Spray one (three) 10-inch Bundt pan(s) with nonstick cooking spray.

Putting the breakfast together

Sprinkle the inside of the pan(s) with granulated sugar to coat. Set aside. In a bowl, combine the flour, baking powder, and salt. In a large bowl, beat the confectioners' sugar and the spread until light and fluffy with a standing mixer. Add the egg substitute, beating until thoroughly incorporated. Beat in the vanilla and almond extracts and the orange zest. Slowly add the flour mixture, beating to incorporate after each addition. Fold the zucchini and cranberries into the batter with a rubber spatula.

For breakfast this morning

Preheat the oven to 350°F. Fill the prepared Bundt pan with batter, dividing it equally among the three pans if you are preparing a triple batch. Alternatively, fill prepared muffin tins in a similar fashion. Bake for 1 hour or until the bread springs back when you press it.

To freeze

Cover with plastic wrap and heavy-duty aluminum foil. Label, date, and freeze for up to 3 months. Thaw at room temperature before baking as directed above.

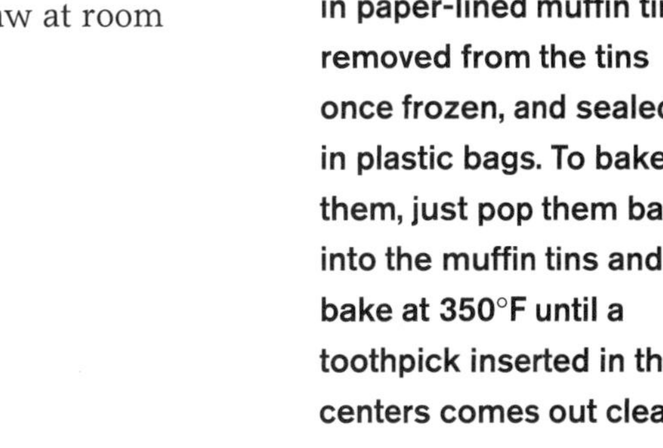

We have found that making many batches of our muffins is a lifesaver—the dough is easily frozen in paper-lined muffin tins, removed from the tins once frozen, and sealed in plastic bags. To bake them, just pop them back into the muffin tins and bake at 350°F until a toothpick inserted in the centers comes out clean.

Ham and Tomato Biscuits

Black Forest ham gives an assertive flavor but any ham will work. Cooked and crumbled bacon is a good substitute.

Serves 6

For One	For Three	Ingredients
		nonstick cooking spray
2 cups	6 cups	all-purpose flour
1 teaspoon	3 teaspoons	dry mustard
1 teaspoon	3 teaspoons	paprika, plus extra for sprinkling
2 teaspoon	6 teaspoons	kosher salt
2 tablespoons	6 tablespoons	baking powder
2 tablespoons	¼ cup plus 2 tablespoons	low-fat yogurt-based spread or butter
1 tablespoon	3 tablespoons	fresh basil, chopped
⅓ cup	1 cup	sun-dried tomatoes packed in oil, drained and chopped
½ cup (3 ounces)	1½ cups (8 ounces)	Black Forest ham, chopped
⅔ cup	2 cups	nonfat milk

Spray one (three) baking sheet(s) with nonstick cooking spray.

Putting the breakfast together

In a bowl, mix together the flour, mustard, paprika, salt, and baking powder. Cut in the spread with two knives or a pastry cutter until the mixture resembles coarse meal. Stir in the basil, sun-dried tomatoes, and ham and mix lightly. Add enough milk to make soft dough. Turn the dough onto a lightly floured surface, knead lightly, and roll out to one (three) 8 × 6-inch rectangle(s). Cut the dough into 2-inch squares and arrange the biscuits on the baking sheet. Brush the top with milk and sprinkle with paprika.

For dinner tonight

Preheat the oven to 400°F. Bake the biscuits for 12 to 15 minutes, until browned around the edges.

To freeze

Bake the biscuits as directed above, cool, and place in resealable freezer bags. To rewarm, preheat the oven to 350°F. Wrap the biscuits in aluminum foil and bake until heated through, 10 to 20 minutes.

Coffee Mocha Punch

Treat your family or guests to a coffee indulgence. Mix together all of the ingredients except the club soda and ice and keep frozen. To serve, partially thaw the mixture and place it in a punch bowl. Add the club soda and ice at the last minute. If you prefer to make this without the coffee liqueur, replace it with an equal amount of coffee. **Serves 6**

For One	For Three	Ingredients
4 cups	12 cups	strong coffee
½ quart	1½ quarts	nonfat vanilla ice cream
½ quart	1½ quarts	nonfat chocolate ice cream
2 cups	6 cups	coffee liqueur such as Kahlúa, optional
½ cup	1½ cups	nonfat milk
¼ cup	¾ cup	sugar
⅛ teaspoon	¼ teaspoon plus ⅛ teaspoon	salt
½ teaspoon	1½ teaspoons	vanilla extract
4 cups	12 cups	crushed ice
½ liter	1½ liters	club soda
¼ teaspoon	¾ teaspoon	ground nutmeg or ground cinnamon, optional

Putting the punch together

Brew the coffee and allow it to cool to room temperature. Scoop the ice cream into a punch bowl using a small ice cream scoop. Pour the coffee over the ice cream. Add the coffee liqueur, milk, sugar, salt, and vanilla and stir gently to incorporate.

For brunch today

Just before serving, add the crushed ice and club soda and garnish with nutmeg or cinnamon.

To freeze

Pour the mixture into resealable freezer bags. Label, date, and freeze for up to 3 months. To serve, partially thaw the mixture and place it in a punch bowl. Add the club soda and ice just before serving and garnish with nutmeg or cinnamon.

Dream Gift

How can you make someone's life easier? Take them a Dream Dinner.

- If your neighbor is taken ill . . .
- For your children's teachers during parent conference week . . .
- For a friend having a baby . . .
- For someone who just moved into a new house . . .
- For someone moving out of her house . . .
- For someone whose spouse is traveling . . .

Berry Freezer Jam

You can use any type of berry or a blend of several different berries for this simple jam. We love raspberry and use it for the filling in Baked Stuffed French Toast on page 46. Make it in the summer when berry season is at its height. This also makes a wonderful gift. **Makes 12 half-pint jars**

For One	For Three	Ingredients
		12 half-pint jars
4 cups	**12 cups**	**berries, picked over and washed**
3 cups	**9 cups**	**sugar**
½ teaspoon	**1½ teaspoons**	**grated lemon zest**
½ cup	**1½ cups**	**freezer jam pectin**
1 tablespoon	**3 tablespoons**	**lemon juice**

Putting the jam together

Inspect the jars, lids, and rings, making sure they are clean and rust free. Place the berries in a large bowl. Crush them in a blender or food processor. Add the sugar and lemon zest. Mix until combined. Let stand for 5 minutes, then add the pectin and lemon juice and mix until incorporated. Ladle the jam into the jars, leaving a ½-inch space at the top of each jar. Place the lids and rings on the jars.

Refrigerate the jars for 24 hours. Label, date, and freeze. The jam tastes best if served after it has been frozen for 3 weeks. It can be frozen for up to 1 year. Use the jam straight from the freezer and refreeze any remaining jam.

Salads, Soups, and Side Dishes

The recipes in this chapter offer up ideas for soups light enough for first courses and hearty enough for dinner itself; salads designed to feed a crowd, and others special enough for an elegant evening at home; and a variety of side dishes to get you through every season. But even better, you could refer to this chapter alone to prepare—and freeze for later—entire meals. Wouldn't it be great to arrive home after a busy day at work and sit down to a dinner of Dreamy French Onion Soup (page 70) and Parmesan Green Beans (page 84) without having to spend precious time in the kitchen? Pull Beef and Cabbage Stew (page 76) from the freezer in the morning and warm it up on the stove when you get home. Serve it with a mixed green salad and a fresh country loaf purchased on your way home, and you'll have time to help the kids with their homework. For a lovely lunch with friends, put together Smoked Turkey and Red Grape Salad (page 60) and serve it with Cremini Mushroom and Caramelized Onion Soup (page 66)—all made ahead and waiting in the freezer. Some of our favorite side dishes are here—Baked Shoestring Potatoes (page 104), Kahlúa Baked Beans (page 98) and Holiday Rice (page 92) among them, and there's even a classic Layered Strawberry Gelatin Salad (page 100) for the buffet table.

Company's Coming Layered Salad

This exquisite salad is a showstopper on a buffet table. It cannot be frozen, but we provide amounts for tripling the recipe so you can easily make it for a crowd. Divide the times-three salad among three clear glass bowls and space them apart on the buffet table. They're as decorative as they are delicious. Serve this salad with Fettuccine with Chicken and Asparagus (page 112).

Serves 6

For One	For Three	Ingredients
1	3	head(s) romaine lettuce, chopped
4	12	celery, chopped
1 cup	3 cups	mushrooms, sliced
6	18	scallions, chopped
1½ cups	4½ cups	frozen peas
1	3	red bell pepper(s), diced
½ cup	1½ cups	bacon bits
2 cups (8 ounces)	6 cups (1½ pounds)	shredded Cheddar cheese
2	6	hard-boiled eggs, chopped
2 cups	6 cups	nonfat mayonnaise

For One	For Three	Ingredients
1 tablespoon	3 tablespoons	packed dark brown sugar
½ teaspoon	1½ teaspoons	kosher salt
½ teaspoon	1½ teaspoons	black pepper
½ teaspoon	1½ teaspoons	garlic powder
1 cup (4 ounces)	3 cups (12 ounces)	crumbled blue cheese or grated Parmesan cheese

Putting the salad together

Place half of the lettuce in a large, clear glass bowl, dividing the lettuce equally among the three bowls if you are preparing a triple batch. Top with the celery, mushrooms, scallions, peas, bell pepper(s), bacon bits, Cheddar cheese, and hard-boiled eggs. Layer the remaining romaine lettuce over the eggs. Set aside.

Mix together the mayonnaise, brown sugar, salt, pepper, and garlic powder in a bowl. Spread this mixture evenly over the top of the salad, dividing it equally if you are preparing a triple batch. Garnish with the blue cheese or Parmesan. Cover with plastic wrap and chill for 8 to 12 hours. Serve.

Modify the recipes to suit your family's tastes—use fewer onions or add more hot sauce, depending on their likes and dislikes.

Smoked Turkey and Red Grape Salad

Yes, you can freeze this salad! Omit the celery if you plan to freeze it and add fresh chopped stalks once the salad is thawed. **Serves 6**

For One	For Three	Ingredients
¼ cup	¾ cup	nonfat sour cream
2 tablespoons	¼ cup plus 2 tablespoons	rice vinegar
¼ cup	¾ cup	nonfat mayonnaise
2 tablespoons	¼ cup plus 2 tablespoons	sugar
1 teaspoon	1 tablespoon	kosher salt
½ teaspoon	1½ teaspoons	black pepper
1⅓ pounds	4 pounds	smoked turkey breast, cut into 1-inch cubes
2 cups (¾ pound)	6 cups (2 pounds)	seedless red grapes
1 cup	3 cups	chopped walnuts
8 ounces	1½ pounds	mozzarella cheese, cut into 1-inch cubes
4	12	celery, diced
1	3	head(s) romaine lettuce, chopped

Putting the salad together

In a bowl, combine the sour cream, vinegar, mayonnaise, sugar, salt, and pepper and mix well. Set aside. Combine the turkey, grapes, walnuts, and cheese in a large bowl. If you are preparing a triple batch, divide the turkey mixture equally among three resealable freezer bags. Pour the sour cream dressing into the bag(s) with the turkey, dividing equally if you are preparing a triple batch. Seal the bag(s) tightly and mix gently.

For salad tonight

Place one bag in the refrigerator for dinner tonight. When ready to serve, add the diced celery to the refrigerated salad mixture and mix gently. Arrange the romaine lettuce on the bottom of a serving dish, place the salad on top, and serve.

To freeze

Label, date, and freeze for up to 3 months. Thaw before serving as directed above.

Spinach and Strawberry Salad

This simple salad of spinach, strawberries, and red onion must be made fresh and never frozen. The dressing recipe can be tripled and will last up to 1 month in the refrigerator. Serve this spring salad with Parmesan-Crusted Fish Fillets (page 210).

Serves 6

For One	For Three	Ingredients
1 pound	3 pounds	fresh spinach
2 cups (1 pint)	6 cups (3 pints)	strawberries, sliced
¼ cup	¾ cup	fresh tarragon, chopped
¼	¾	small red onion, thinly sliced
2 tablespoons	¼ cup plus 2 tablespoons	balsamic vinegar
1 tablespoon	3 tablespoons	honey
1½ tablespoons	¼ cup	olive oil
½ teaspoon	1½ teaspoons	lemon juice
½ teaspoon	1½ teaspoons	dried tarragon
½ teaspoon	1½ teaspoons	kosher salt
½ teaspoon	1½ teaspoons	black pepper
½ cup (2 ounces)	1½ cups (6 ounces)	almonds, sliced

Putting the salad together

In a large bowl, combine the spinach, strawberries, fresh tarragon, and onion. Toss to mix well. Set aside. In a jar with a lid, combine the vinegar, honey, olive oil, lemon juice, dried tarragon, salt, pepper, and 1 (3) tablespoon(s) water. Screw the lid on tightly and shake to mix well. Pour the dressing over the salad just before serving, dividing the dressing equally if you are preparing a triple batch. Toss to coat. Garnish with the almonds and serve.

Let's Talk

Ask the questions that will get even teenagers to talk:

What do you think is the biggest controversy in your school?

How can you make a difference?

Who and how did you serve (do something for someone) today?

What was the craziest thing you saw on the roads today?

Orzo Salad

Pasta salad with a Greek twist. After thawing this salad, splash a little balsamic vinegar on it right before serving. Intensely flavorful ingredients including olives, scallions, feta, and dill make this pasta salad an especially good one.

Serves 6

For One	For Three	Ingredients
1 cup (4 ounces)	3 cups (12 ounces)	orzo (uncooked)
6	18	scallions, chopped
½ cup (4 ounces)	1½ cups (12 ounces)	pitted and chopped Kalamata olives
½ cup (2 ounces)	1½ cups (6 ounces)	crumbled feta cheese
¼ cup	¾ cup	chopped fresh dill
¼ cup	¾ cup	olive oil
3 tablespoons	½ cup plus 1 tablespoon	lemon juice
1 teaspoon	1 tablespoon	grated lemon zest
¼ cup	¾ cup	red wine vinegar
1 teaspoon	1 tablespoon	kosher salt
1 teaspoon	1 tablespoon	black pepper

Lemon or lime zest brightens the flavor in almost any dish.

Putting the salad together

Cook the orzo according to the package directions. In a large bowl, combine the orzo, scallions, olives, feta, and dill. Set aside.

In a small bowl, whisk together the olive oil, lemon juice and zest, vinegar, salt, and pepper.

Pour over the pasta mixture and stir to coat all over. Divide the remaining salad equally between two resealable freezer bags if you are preparing a triple batch.

For dinner tonight

Transfer the pasta salad to a serving dish and serve.

To freeze

Label, date, and freeze for up to 3 months. Thaw before serving as directed above.

Let's talk

One of our favorite conversation starters that involves everyone at the table is the Pow and Wow Game. Each diner has to share a story of either a really good thing that happened to them (Wow!) or a really bad thing that happened to them (Pow!).

Cremini Mushroom and Caramelized Onion Soup

Flavorful brown cremini mushrooms are simply a small version of portobello mushrooms. Do not substitute button mushrooms for them in this recipe as they are nowhere near as rich in flavor. If you like, puree the cooked soup in a blender for a smooth first course. **Serves 6**

For One	For Three	Ingredients
		nonstick cooking spray
2 cups (8 ounces)	6 cups (1½ pounds)	cremini mushrooms, sliced
4 cups	12 cups	yellow onions, thinly sliced
2 tablespoons	¼ cup plus 2 tablespoons	sugar
4 cups	12 cups	chicken broth
2 tablespoons	¼ cup plus 2 tablespoons	chopped fresh rosemary
1 teaspoon	1 tablespoon	kosher salt
½ teaspoon	1½ teaspoons	black pepper

Putting the soup together

Heat a large skillet over high heat and spray with nonstick cooking spray. Add half of the mushrooms, the onions, and sugar and sauté, stirring every 3 to 5 minutes, until the onions are browned and tender, about 15 minutes. Add the chicken broth, the remaining mushrooms, the rosemary, salt, and pepper and stir until combined. Transfer the mixture to a large pot. If you are preparing a triple batch, pour one-third into the pot and divide the remainder equally between two resealable freezer bags.

For dinner tonight

Turn the heat to low and simmer the soup on the stove for 1 hour, stirring often.

To freeze

Label, date, and freeze for up to 3 months. Thaw at room temperature before cooking as directed above.

Kielbasa Bean Soup

This hearty soup is a meal in itself. Use low-fat turkey kielbasa to lighten this fiber-rich dinner.

Serves 6

For One	For Three	Ingredients
2 cups (8 ounces)	6 cups (1½ pounds)	potatoes in ½-inch dice
2	6	10.5-ounce can(s) bean with bacon soup
2	6	15-ounce can(s) diced tomatoes
¾ pound	2 pounds	kielbasa sausage, cut into 1-inch pieces
1	3	onion(s), chopped
2	6	carrots, diced
2	6	celery, diced
1 teaspoon	1 tablespoon	kosher salt
½ teaspoon	1½ teaspoons	black pepper

Kids are creatures of habit. It takes up to six months to change their eating habits, so be patient—they will come around and they'll be better eaters in the long run, and healthier children, too.

Putting the soup together

In a large bowl, combine the potatoes, soup, tomatoes, kielbasa, onion(s), carrots, celery, salt, and pepper and stir to combine. Transfer to a crockpot or large pot. If you are preparing a triple batch, transfer one-third to a stockpot and divide the remainder equally between two resealable freezer bags.

For dinner tonight

Slow-cook in the crockpot, set on low heat, for 5 to 6 hours, until thick. Alternatively, simmer over low heat on the stovetop for 2 hours or until thick.

To freeze

Place each resealable freezer bag into a second one and seal tightly. Label, date, and freeze for up to 3 months. Thaw at room temperature before cooking as directed above.

For truly fuss-free meals, use your crockpot. Not only does cooking slowly over low heat result in the most tender pieces of meat but you will arrive home to a wonderful aroma in your kitchen, one that suggests you've been cooking all day!

Dreamy French Onion Soup

Caramelizing onions is well worth the wait—so don't rush the process that results in these melt-in-your-mouth onions. The natural sugars in the onions become concentrated, causing the onions to brown, yet remain soft. You can use low-sodium beef broth for this recipe. We mix Merlot with the beef stock to make a full-bodied broth, but any decent red will do.

Serves 6

For One	For Three	Ingredients
8	24	onions, thinly sliced
¼ cup	¾ cup	olive oil
2 tablespoons	¼ cup plus 2 tablespoons	granulated sugar
10½ cups	2 gallons	beef broth
1 teaspoon	3 teaspoons	kosher salt
1 cup	3 cups	red wine
6	18	sourdough bread (sliced to fit bowls), toasted
6 slices (4 ounces)	18 slices (12 ounces)	Gruyère cheese
½ cup (2 ounces)	1½ cups (6 ounces)	grated Parmesan cheese
½ cup (2 ounces)	1½ cups (6 ounces)	grated Fontina cheese
1 tablespoon	3 tablespoons	chives, chopped
leaves from 1 sprig	leaves from 3 sprigs	thyme

Putting the soup together

Heat a skillet over medium-low heat. Add the onions, olive oil, and sugar and cook until the onions are dark brown, about 40 minutes, stirring them in the pan frequently as they begin to take on color. Raise the heat to high, add the broth, and bring to a boil. Reduce the heat to medium-low and simmer, uncovered, for 10 to 20 minutes. Add the salt and wine. If you are preparing a triple batch, divide two-thirds of the broth and onion mixture equally between two resealable freezer bags and seal.

Pick one day a week and encourage your family to invite friends over for dinner and start a wonderful tradition.

For dinner tonight

Preheat the broiler. Ladle the soup from the pot into six heat-proof bowls. Float a slice of sourdough bread on top of the soup. Place a slice of Gruyère on each bread slice, then sprinkle with Parmesan and Fontina. Cook under the broiler and broil until the cheese is melted, bubbling, and begins to brown. Garnish with chives and thyme.

To freeze

Place 6 slices of bread in each of two resealable freezer bags. Divide the Gruyère, Parmesan, and Fontina equally between two resealable freezer bags. Label, date, and freeze for up to 2 months. Thaw at room temperature before cooking as directed above.

Seafood Cioppino

There's little work to do but chop some onions, celery, and garlic. You can substitute a variety of fresh fish for the halibut, such as cod. If you prefer to cook this on the stovetop, simmer it for at least 30 minutes, until it is heated through, then add the seafood and simmer for 5 minutes more for a hearty meal.

Serves 6

For One	For Three	Ingredients
1	3	onion(s), diced
2	6	celery, chopped
2 teaspoons	2 tablespoons	minced garlic
1	3	28-ounce can(s) diced tomatoes
1 cup	3 cups	chicken broth
1 cup	3 cups	clam juice
⅓ cup	1 cup	tomato paste
½ cup	1½ cups	red wine
2 tablespoons	¼ cup plus 2 tablespoons	red wine vinegar
2 tablespoons	¼ cup plus 2 tablespoons	olive oil
1 teaspoon	1 tablespoon	kosher salt
1 teaspoon	1 tablespoon	black pepper

For One	For Three	Ingredients
zest of 1	zest of 3	lemon(s), grated
2 teaspoons	2 tablespoons	Italian seasoning
1 tablespoon	3 tablespoons	sugar
¼ teaspoon	¾ teaspoon	red pepper flakes
1	3	bay leaf (leaves)
6 ounces	1 pound, 2 ounces	skinless halibut fillets, cut into 3 (9) pieces
6	18	large shrimp, 21 to 30 per pound, peeled and deveined
1	3	6-ounce can(s) chopped clams, drained
1 cup	3 cups	crabmeat, canned or fresh, picked over and drained
2 tablespoons	¼ cup plus 2 tablespoons	lemon juice
2 tablespoons	¼ cup plus 2 tablespoons	dried parsley

Putting the dinner together

In a large bowl, combine the onion(s), celery, garlic, tomatoes, chicken broth, clam juice, tomato paste, red wine, red wine vinegar, olive oil, salt, pepper, lemon zest, Italian seasoning, sugar, red pepper flakes, and bay leaf. Mix to incorporate. Pour the mixture into a crockpot or a large pot. If you are preparing a triple batch, pour one-third of the mixture into the pot and divide the remaining mixture equally between two resealable freezer bags. Combine the halibut, shrimp, clams, crabmeat, lemon juice, and parsley in a resealable freezer bag and refrigerate. If you are preparing a triple batch, divide the fish equally among three resealable freezer bags.

For dinner tonight

Cook the vegetables and broth on low heat in your crockpot for 5 to 6 hours, or simmer on the stovetop for 1 to 2 hours. Add the seafood, stir gently, and cook on low heat for another 5 to 10 minutes or until the fish breaks apart and just until the shrimp turns pink.

To freeze

Place one bag of vegetables and broth inside each bag of seafood and seal tightly. Label, date, and freeze for up to 3 months. Thaw at room temperature before cooking as directed above.

When cutting up vegetables, dice them into 1-inch pieces. They will freeze well and reheat better than smaller pieces.

Simple, Fresh Vegetable and Fruit Side Dishes in 5 Minutes or Less

Tomatoes: Cut into thick slices and drizzle with your favorite olive oil and vinegar or salad dressing. Sprinkle with fresh chopped herbs.

Cucumbers: Slice and marinate in seasoned rice vinegar for 1 to 6 hours.

Broccoli: Cut into spears and place in a microwave-safe dish. Dot with yogurt-based spread and sprinkle with lemon pepper. Cover with plastic wrap and microwave on high for 2 to 3 minutes, until fork tender.

Asparagus: Place the spears on a baking sheet, drizzle with nonfat Italian dressing, and cook under the broiler for 2 minutes.

Baby carrots: Place in a microwave-safe dish, sprinkle with brown sugar, a pinch of cayenne, and a dollop of yogurt-based spread, cover with plastic wrap, and microwave on high for 1 to 2 minutes.

Red and green bell peppers: Cut into rings and drizzle with nonfat Italian dressing.

Melons: Slice and arrange attractively on a platter. Drizzle with honey, if desired.

Fresh fruit of any kind: Serve on a lettuce leaf and drizzle with balsamic vinegar.

Beef and Cabbage Stew

This hearty stew, thick with beef, beans, and cabbage, makes a delicious dinner on a cold winter day, and is even better the next day once the flavors have melded. You can omit the beans if you like. If you prefer a souplike consistency, add an extra cup of broth and tomato sauce. If you are preparing a triple batch, you will need two soup pots unless you have one that can accommodate 3 gallons of liquid. **Serves 6**

For One	For Three	Ingredients
1½ pounds	4½ pounds	lean ground beef
5	15	celery, diced
½	1½	onion, diced
dash	3 dashes	Tabasco sauce
¼ teaspoon	¾ teaspoon	chili powder
1	3	28-ounce can(s) diced tomatoes with juice
1¼ cups	3¾ cups	beef broth
2	6	15-ounce can(s) kidney beans, drained
1	3	15-ounce can(s) tomato sauce
1 teaspoon	3 teaspoons	kosher salt
½ teaspoon	1½ teaspoons	black pepper

For One	For Three	Ingredients
½	1½	**head(s) cabbage, cut into 1-inch wedges**
1 cup	3 cups	**chopped fresh parsley**
½ cup (2 ounces)	1½ cups (6 ounces)	**grated Parmesan cheese**

Putting the stew together

In a large skillet over medium-high heat, combine the beef, celery, and onion, season with Tabasco and chili powder and sauté until the beef is browned, 8 to 10 minutes for 1½ pounds and 18 to 20 minutes for 4½ pounds. Transfer the mixture to a soup pot and set over high heat. Add the tomatoes, broth, beans, tomato sauce, salt, pepper, and cabbage and bring to a boil. Reduce the heat to medium and simmer for at least 1 hour. If you are preparing a triple batch, cool the remaining mixture in the refrigerator and divide equally between two resealable freezer bags.

For dinner tonight

Ladle the stew into six soup bowls and garnish each with 2 tablespoons of the parsley and 1 tablespoon of the Parmesan.

To freeze

Combine 1 cup of the parsley and ½ cup of the Parmesan in each of two resealable freezer bags. Label, date, and freeze along with the stew for up to 3 months. Thaw, reheat, and serve as directed above.

Seafood Chowder

Trying to add more seafood and vegetables to your diet? Soups are the perfect way to include both.

Serves 6

For One	For Three	Ingredients
½ cup	1½ cups	low-fat yogurt-based spread or butter
3 tablespoons	⅔ cup	all-purpose flour
⅓	1	onion, diced
⅓	1	red bell pepper, diced
⅓	1	yellow bell pepper, diced
1 cup	3 cups	dry white wine
1 quart	3 quarts	nonfat half-and-half
2 tablespoons	6 tablespoons	chicken bouillon powder or cubes
1½ teaspoons	1¼ tablespoons	dried thyme
⅓ cup	1 cup	frozen whole-kernel corn, thawed
1 cup (4 ounces)	3 cups (12 ounces)	cooked new potatoes, diced
1 teaspoon	3 teaspoons	kosher salt
1 teaspoon	3 teaspoons	white or black pepper
4	12	asparagus spears, cut into 1-inch pieces

For One	For Three	Ingredients
3 ounces	9 ounces	fresh crabmeat, picked over
4 ounces	12 ounces	Bay shrimp, peeled and deveined
1 teaspoon	3 teaspoons	chives, chopped

Putting the soup together

Melt the spread in a large soup pot over medium heat. Add the flour and stir until slightly browned. Add the onion and sauté until the flour is golden brown, 8 to 10 minutes. Add the bell peppers and cook until slightly tender, 5 to 8 minutes. Blend in the wine and add the half-and-half slowly, stirring constantly. Continuing to stir constantly, bring the mixture to a simmer. Add the chicken bouillon, thyme, corn, potatoes, salt, and pepper. Stirring occasionally, simmer until the potatoes are warmed through and the chowder is thickened, about 1 hour. Season with salt and pepper. Add the asparagus and simmer on low for 10 to 12 minutes or until the asparagus is tender.

For dinner tonight

Bring the chowder to a boil and add the crabmeat and shrimp, ladle into bowls or cups, garnish with chives, and serve immediately.

To freeze

Pour the chowder into resealable freezer bags, placing the seafood in separate bags. Label, date, and freeze for up to 3 months. Thaw the chowder and seafood in the refrigerator before cooking as directed above.

Three Cheese Spinach Soup

Use fresh or frozen spinach for this thick, warming soup. Serve it with Ham and Tomato Biscuits (page 52) for lunch or a light supper. **Serves 6**

For One	For Three	Ingredients
¼ cup	¾ cup	low-fat yogurt-based spread or butter
5 tablespoons	1 cup	all-purpose flour
1 cup	3 cups	button mushrooms, sliced
1	3	scallion(s), chopped
2 cups	6 cups	chicken broth
2 cups	6 cups	nonfat milk
1 cup (8 ounces)	3 cups (1½ pounds)	nonfat cream cheese
1 cup (4 ounces)	3 cups (12 ounces)	shredded Swiss cheese
4 teaspoons	¾ teaspoons	ground nutmeg
½ teaspoon	1½ teaspoons	kosher salt
1 teaspoon	3 teaspoons	black pepper
1	3	10-ounce box(es) frozen chopped spinach, thawed and drained
¼ cup (1 ounce)	¾ cup (3 ounces)	grated Parmesan cheese

Putting the soup together

Melt the spread in a large soup pot over medium heat. Add the flour and whisk until golden, 2 to 3 minutes. Add the mushrooms and scallion(s) and sauté until tender, about 3 minutes. Whisk in the chicken broth and milk and stir until thickened, 5 to 10 minutes. Add the cream cheese, Swiss cheese, nutmeg, salt, and pepper and stir until the cheese is melted. Add the spinach and stir. Simmer the soup for 10 to 15 minutes, stirring gently. If you are preparing a triple batch, divide the remaining soup equally between two resealable freezer bags.

For dinner tonight

Ladle the soup from the pot into six bowls. Garnish with ¼ cup of the Parmesan and serve hot.

To freeze

Place ¼ cup Parmesan into each of two resealable bags. Label, date, and freeze both the soup and the Parmesan for up to 3 months. Thaw at room temperature before cooking as directed above.

Five-Spice Grilled Chicken

These five spices coat the chicken, sealing in the moisture while adding a layer of flavor. Serve this with the Lemon Rice Pilaf on page 86 and tossed greens for a wonderfully simple dinner.

Serves 6

For One	For Three	Ingredients
6	18	4-ounce boneless, skinless chicken breasts
2 tablespoons	6 tablespoons	ground cumin
2 tablespoons	6 tablespoons	chili powder
2 tablespoons	6 tablespoons	packed light brown sugar
2 tablespoons	6 tablespoons	curry powder
2 teaspoons	6 teaspoons	kosher salt
2 teaspoons	6 teaspoons	black pepper

Putting your dinner together

Place 6 chicken breasts into a 1-gallon resealable freezer bag. Sprinkle each seasoning over the chicken and seal tightly. Toss the bag to coat the chicken breasts.

For dinner tonight

Marinate the chicken in the refrigerator for at least 1 hour. Heat a grill to medium-high. Grill the chicken for 5 to 8 minutes per side. Or, heat a non-stick skillet sprayed with cooking spray over medium-high heat. Add the chicken breasts and brown for 3 minutes on each side. Reduce to medium heat and cook for 5 to 8 minutes per side.

To freeze

Divide the seasoned chicken breasts into thirds and place in resealable freezer bags. Label, date, and freeze for up to 3 months. Thaw before cooking as directed above.

Let's Talk

Inevitably, difficult subjects or disagreements will arise that are certain to stop conversation dead. Rather than put a halt to talking, indulge it in a rational way, by asking everyone to discuss the pros and cons on the subject, examine the consequences of the varying viewpoints, and ultimately respectfully agree that it is okay to disagree. If the conversation takes a further negative turn, defer the discussion until after dinner.

Parmesan Green Beans

As a side dish or appetizer these beans are transformed into a delicious treat. Sauté or roast them in your oven to make them extra special.

Serves 6

For One	For Three	Ingredients
2 tablespoons	¼ cup plus 2 tablespoons	olive oil
1 tablespoon	3 tablespoons	minced garlic
1	3	scallion(s), chopped
1	3	red, yellow, or green bell pepper(s), chopped
1 teaspoon	1 tablespoon	dried basil
1 teaspoon	1 tablespoon	kosher salt
½ teaspoon	1½ teaspoons	black pepper
1	3	20-ounce package(s) frozen green beans
¼ cup (2 ounces)	¾ cup (6 ounces)	grated Parmesan cheese

Putting the dish together

In a bowl, combine the olive oil, garlic, scallion(s), bell pepper(s), basil, salt, and pepper. If you are preparing a triple batch, divide the pepper mixture equally between two resealable freezer bags. Place the green beans in a separate resealable freezer bag. Place the Parmesan in a smaller bag. Bag all three (seasoning bag, bean bag, and cheese bag) together.

For dinner tonight

Heat a large skillet over medium-high heat. Add the pepper mixture and sauté until fragrant, about 5 minutes. Add the green beans and ½ cup water and simmer until the beans are bright green and tender, about 8 minutes. Transfer to a platter, sprinkle with the Parmesan, and serve.

To freeze

Place ¼ cup of the Parmesan in each of two resealable freezer bags. Label, date, and freeze both the cheese and the vegetables for up to 3 months. Thaw at room temperature before cooking as directed above.

Optional way to cook

Toss the beans in the olive oil, garlic, basil, salt, and pepper. Remove the beans, arrange in a single layer on a baking sheet, and roast at 475°F until browned, about 10 minutes. Place the roasted beans on a serving platter. Sprinkle with grated Parmesan.

Lemon Rice Pilaf

The fresh lemon juice in this rice dish gives it a slight tang, making it the perfect accompaniment to seafood. Make a triple batch and bring it along on a seaside vacation. Bake it in the oven, put the fish on the grill, and enjoy a delicious meal in minutes.

Serves 6 to 8

For One	For Three	Ingredients
5 tablespoons	¾ cup plus 3 tablespoons	olive oil
1½	4½	onions, chopped
3 cups	9 cups	uncooked long-grain rice
5 cups	15 cups	chicken broth
½ cup	1½ cups	freshly squeezed lemon juice
1½ tablespoons	¼ cup plus ½ tablespoon	lemon zest
½ teaspoon	1½ teaspoons	kosher salt
¾ teaspoon	2¼ teaspoons	black pepper

Putting the dish together

Heat the oil in a large saucepan over medium heat. Add the onions and sauté until tender and fragrant, about 5 minutes. Add the rice and sauté for 2 minutes more.

Raise the heat to high, add the chicken broth, lemon juice and zest, salt, and pepper and bring to a boil, stirring occasionally. Reduce the heat to low. Cover and cook until the rice is tender and the liquid is absorbed, about 20 minutes.

For dinner tonight

Remove from the heat and let stand for 5 minutes. Fluff with a fork and serve.

To freeze

Divide the remaining rice equally between two 2-quart baking dishes, and cover with plastic wrap and aluminum foil. Label, date, and freeze. Thaw. Preheat the oven to 350°F. Add ½ cup water or chicken stock and bake, covered, for 40 minutes or until the liquid is absorbed.

It is better to undercook, or cook just until tender, all types of rice to be used in freezable dinners. They will finish cooking when dinner is reheated.

Cajun Dirty Rice

This recipe comes from an old friend of ours who was a cook in New Orleans. We never could get him to write it down exactly, but don't be afraid of all the ingredients; it is a wonderfully seasoned dish to have on hand.

Serves 6

For One	For Three	Ingredients
1½ cups	4½ cups	uncooked long grain white rice
4	12	slices of cooked bacon, crumbled
½ pound	1½ pounds	sausages, cooked and crumbled
½ cup	1½ cups	yellow onions, diced
½ cup	1½ cups	celery, diced
½ cup	1½ cups	green bell pepper(s), diced
½ cup	1½ cups	red bell pepper(s), diced
1 tablespoons	3 tablespoons	minced garlic
¼ cup	¾ cup	prepared red pepper pesto
½ teaspoon	1½ teaspoons	cayenne powder
1 tablespoon	3 tablespoons	dried parsley
1 tablespoon	3 tablespoons	granulated sugar
1 teaspoon	3 teaspoons	kosher salt

For One	For Three	Ingredients
1 teaspoon	3 teaspoons	black pepper
1 cup	3 cups	chicken broth
¼ cup	¾ cup	olive oil

Putting your dinner together

Cook the rice according to the package directions and cool in the refrigerator. Place the remaining ingredients in a 1-gallon resealable freezer bag and mix in the cooled rice. Toss the bag to coat the rice. Repeat in separate bags if you are preparing a triple batch.

For dinner tonight

Place the contents in a sprayed baking dish and cover tightly. Bake in a 350°F oven for 1 hour or until the liquid is fully absorbed and the rice is hot and fluffy.

To freeze

Label, date, and freeze for up to 3 months. Thaw before cooking as directed above.

Wild Rice Salad

This is the perfect make-ahead dish for Thanksgiving or any time during the cooler months, when a hearty side dish is most appreciated. It is especially delicious with the Provençal Flank Steak (page 140). **Serves 6**

For One	For Three	Ingredients
¼ cup	¾ cup	uncooked wild rice
1¼ cups	3¾ cups	uncooked brown rice
1	3	Granny Smith apple(s)
1 tablespoon	3 tablespoons	lemon juice
½ cup	1½ cups	red bell pepper(s), diced
½ cup	1½ cups	dried cranberries
½ cup (2 ounces)	1½ cups (6 ounces)	pecans, chopped and toasted
¼	¾	red onion, chopped
2 tablespoons	¼ cup plus 2 tablespoons	balsamic vinegar
¼ cup	¾ cup	olive oil
1 teaspoon	1 tablespoon	kosher salt
½ teaspoon	1½ teaspoons	black pepper

Putting the dish together

Cook the wild rice and the brown rice in separate saucepans, following the package directions. Cool the rice uncovered in a 2-inch-deep container on the top shelf of the refrigerator. Core the apple(s), slice, cut into 1-inch pieces, and toss with lemon juice in a large bowl. Add the rice, bell pepper(s), cranberries, pecans, and onion and mix to combine. Set aside.

In a small bowl, whisk together the vinegar, oil, salt, and pepper. Add the dressing to the rice mixture and stir to combine. If you are preparing a triple batch, divide the remaining salad equally between two resealable freezer bags.

For dinner tonight

Transfer to a platter, fluff with a fork, and serve.

To freeze

Label, date, and freeze for up to 3 months. Thaw before serving as directed above. A splash of balsamic vinegar will freshen this salad up perfectly.

Holiday Rice

You still have the turkey to roast, the potatoes to mash, and the yams to bake, but your rice is done. So go ahead and pull your Pecan Pie (page 236) out of the freezer and serve a comfortable, easy holiday dinner.

Serves 6

For One	For Three	Ingredients
		nonstick cooking spray
1 cup	3 cups	uncooked wild rice
1 cup	3 cups	uncooked brown rice
1 cup	3 cups	dried cranberries
½ cup (3 ounces)	1½ cups (9 ounces)	pine nuts, toasted
¼ cup	¾ cup	fresh parsley, chopped
¼ cup	¾ cup	olive oil
grated zest and juice of 1	grated zest and juice of 3	orange(s)
1 teaspoon	1 tablespoon	kosher salt
½ teaspoon	1½ teaspoons	black pepper
½ cup (2 ounces)	1½ cups (6 ounces)	grated Parmesan cheese

Spray one (three) 9 × 13-inch baking dish(es) with nonstick cooking spray.

Putting the dish together

Cook the wild rice according to the package directions or until the rice is chewy. Drain if necessary. Transfer the rice to a large bowl. Meanwhile, cook the brown rice according to the package directions. Add the wild rice to the brown rice in the large pot. Add the cranberries, pine nuts, parsley, olive oil, orange juice and zest, salt, and pepper. Stir to mix well. Transfer to the prepared baking dish, dividing equally among the three dishes if you are preparing a triple batch.

For dinner tonight

Preheat the oven to 350°F. Cover the rice mixture with aluminum foil and bake for 20 to 30 minutes, until the rice is soft but not mushy. Sprinkle with Parmesan and serve.

To freeze

Cover the baking dishes with plastic wrap and heavy-duty aluminum foil. Place ½ cup of the Parmesan in each of two resealable freezer bags. Label, date, and freeze the rice and cheese for up to 3 months. Thaw before cooking as directed above.

Green and White Bean Salad

This bicolor bean salad is among the fastest to put together in the Dream Dinners repertoire. We like to use Great Northern beans, but cannellini beans will work beautifully, too. Don't bother to thaw the frozen green beans if you are going to freeze this salad; thaw them only when you are ready to serve it.

Serves 6

For One	For Three	Ingredients
1	3	16-ounce bag(s) frozen green beans, thawed
2	6	16-ounce can(s) white beans, such as Great Northern or cannellini beans, drained
4 teaspoons	¼ cup	minced garlic
1	3	red bell pepper(s), thinly sliced
½ cup	1½ cups	fat-free Italian dressing
2 tablespoons	6 tablespoons	balsamic vinegar
½ teaspoon	1½ teaspoons	kosher salt
½ teaspoon	1½ teaspoons	black pepper
1 cup (4 ounces)	3 cups (12 ounces)	grated Parmesan cheese
½ cup	1½ cups	fresh parsley, chopped

Putting the salad together

Combine the green and white beans, garlic, bell pepper(s), Italian dressing, balsamic vinegar, salt, and pepper in a large bowl. Combine the cheese and parsley in another bowl. If you are preparing a triple batch, divide the bean mixture into three equal portions, reserving one portion for tonight. Place the other two portions into two resealable freezer bags. Divide the cheese mixture accordingly, placing one-third each into separate resealable freezer bags.

For dinner tonight

Toss the cheese and the bean mixtures together in a large bowl. Transfer to a serving bowl.

To freeze

Slide a bag of the cheese mixture into each of the bags with the bean mixture. Label, date, and freeze for up to 3 months. Thaw before serving as directed above.

Black Bean and Rice Salad

With Southwestern flavors of salsa, lime juice, and cilantro, this salad pairs perfectly with the Raspberry Margarita Slush (page 28) for a casual but festive dinner. Freezing this salad will soften the vegetables, but it will still have the same wonderful flavors. **Serves 6**

For One	For Three	Ingredients
1 cup	3 cups	uncooked rice, cooked and chilled
1 16-ounce bag	3 16-ounce bags	frozen corn kernels
1	3	15-ounce can(s) black beans, drained
4	12	tomatoes, chopped
1	3	red bell pepper(s), thinly sliced
1 cup	3 cups	cilantro, chopped, plus 1 bunch for garnish
½ teaspoon	1½ teaspoons	red pepper flakes
1 teaspoon	1 tablespoon	oregano
1 tablespoon	3 tablespoons	sugar
½ teaspoon	1½ teaspoons	kosher salt
1 teaspoon	3 teaspoons	minced garlic
3	9	scallions, chopped
1 cup	3 cups	lemon juice

For One	For Three	Ingredients
¼ cup	¾ cup	lime juice
2 tablespoons	¼ cup plus 2 tablespoons	olive oil
½ cup	1½ cups	store-bought salsa (for extra zing, use the salsa on page 20)
		nonfat sour cream for garnish

Putting the salad together

Cook the rice according to the package directions and chill. Place the cooked rice in a large bowl. Add the corn, black beans, tomatoes, bell pepper(s), cilantro, red pepper flakes, oregano, sugar, salt, garlic, and scallions to the rice and toss to mix. In a small bowl, whisk together the lemon juice, lime juice, olive oil, and salsa. Pour the mixture over the rice and toss to mix well. If you are preparing a triple batch, divide the salad into three equal portions, reserving one for tonight; place the other two into two resealable freezer bags.

Make life easier; use chopped garlic in the jar.

For dinner tonight

Refrigerate the salad for 6 to 8 hours. Garnish with dollops of nonfat sour cream and fresh chopped cilantro and serve.

To freeze

Label, date, and freeze for up to 3 months. Thaw, garnish with cilantro, and serve with sour cream.

Kahlúa Baked Beans

These baked beans taste best if they are allowed to marinate in the coffee liqueur and molasses sauce overnight. Thaw frozen beans in the refrigerator for a day or two before cooking. **Serves 6**

For One	For Three	Ingredients
¾ pound	2¼ pounds	cooked ground beef
2	6	28-ounce can(s) baked beans
1	3	yellow onion(s), diced
1 cup	3 cups	coffee liqueur, such as Kahlúa
¼ cup	¾ cup	mild chili sauce
2 tablespoons	¼ cup plus 2 tablespoons	prepared yellow mustard
2 tablespoons	¼ cup plus 2 tablespoons	molasses

Putting the dish together

In a large bowl, combine the ingredients and stir to mix. If you are preparing a triple batch, divide the beans and sauce equally among three resealable freezer bags. Place each in a second resealable freezer bag.

For dinner tonight

Let the beans marinate for 6 to 8 hours or overnight. Preheat the oven to 350°F. Put the beans in an ovenproof casserole, cover with aluminum foil, and bake for 45 to 60 minutes. Uncover and bake for 30 minutes more, or until bubbly and the edges are crusty. Alternatively, slow-cook in a crockpot on low heat for 5 to 6 hours.

To freeze

Label, date, and freeze for up to 3 months. Thaw in the refrigerator before cooking as directed above.

10-Minute Side Dishes

If fresh vegetables are not available, you can still make fresh-tasting, almost-from-scratch side dishes using canned or boxed items that are readily available in every supermarket. Some of our favorites include:

Canned baked beans with sautéed scallions.

Canned green beans steamed and seasoned with lemon pepper.

Canned corn steamed in the canned liquids and seasoned with dried tarragon.

Refried beans warmed and topped with grated cheese.

Boxed pastas and sauces, cooked and placed in a baking dish, sprinkled with grated cheese and Italian seasoning, and placed under the broiler until the cheese is bubbly.

Minute rice steamed and tossed with:

a can of diced tomatoes and garnished with chopped scallions

lemon pepper, lemon zest and juice

applesauce, diced red onion, and curry powder

Couscous cooked and fluffed, then tossed with a handful of grated cheese, cooked frozen peas, and seasoned with kosher salt and pepper.

Layered Strawberry Gelatin Salad

This light, refreshing crowd-pleaser is not only delicious but also colorful on a buffet or the dinner table. This salad can't be frozen, but it can be prepared 2 days ahead.

Serves 6

For One	For Three	Ingredients
1	3	18-ounce box(es) strawberry gelatin
2	6	10-ounce boxes frozen strawberries
1	3	8-ounce can(s) crushed pineapple, drained
2	6	ripe bananas, mashed
½ cup	1½ cups	nonfat sour cream

Putting the salad together

Bring 2 (6) cups water to a boil and add 1 (3) package(s) Jell-O. Add the frozen strawberries, pineapple, and bananas. Put half of the mixture in a 9 × 13-inch baking dish, or divide equally among the three dishes if you are preparing a triple batch. Chill in the refrigerator for 30 to 60 minutes (leave the other half of the mixture out on the counter).

Remove the baking dish(es) from the refrigerator and spread with sour cream. Pour the remaining mixture over the sour cream, dividing equally among the three dishes if you are preparing a triple batch.

For dinner tonight

Cover the dishes with plastic wrap and chill for 8 to 12 hours. Remove the plastic wrap and serve.

Our Daily Bread

There's nothing like the aroma of fresh bread lingering in the kitchen, but when time is at a premium—and a visit to the local bakery isn't an option—you can make delicious bread quickly from easy-to-find items at the grocery store.

Canned brown bread: warm as directed, slice and spread with low-fat yogurt-based spread or butter.

Focaccia: brush with olive oil, sprinkle with Italian seasoning and kosher salt, and broil until browned.

French bread: split lengthwise, spread with low-fat yogurt-based spread or unsalted butter on one side and sprinkle with kosher garlic salt, then spread with cream cheese on the other. Wrap in aluminum foil and bake at 350°F for 10 to 20 minutes, until the cream cheese has melted.

Canned refrigerator biscuits: arrange in a baking pan, spread with low-fat yogurt-based spread or butter, sprinkle with kosher garlic salt and Italian seasoning, then bake as directed.

For soup bowl sourdough: hollow out small rounds of sourdough, leaving a 1-inch wall, and use to serve soups, stews, and chili.

For quick homemade bread: combine 3 cups self-rising flour, 3 tablespoons sugar, and 1 can beer in a bowl. Spread into a loaf pan. Pour ½ cup (1 stick) melted low-fat yogurt-based spread or unsalted butter over the dough and bake at 350°F for 1 hour or until set. Let the bread cool in the pan for 5 minutes, slice, and serve.

Corn Bread Muffins

Freezing these muffins before baking them allows you to bake them as needed. You'll be ready for a crowd or an intimate dinner for two. These are wonderful spread with a simple honey-yogurt-based spread (a combination of equal parts honey and low-fat yogurt-based spread or unsalted butter whipped together). Serve the muffins alongside Chicken and Black Bean Chili (page 196).

Makes 12 muffins

For One	For Three	Ingredients
1 cup	3 cups	all-purpose flour
1 cup	3 cups	yellow cornmeal
2 tablespoons	¼ cup plus 2 tablespoons	sugar
2 teaspoons	2 tablespoons	baking powder
1 teaspoon	3 teaspoons	baking soda
½ cup	1½ cups	nonfat egg substitute
1 cup	3 cups	low-fat buttermilk
3 tablespoons	½ cup plus 1 tablespoon	vegetable oil

Line one (three) 12-muffin pan(s) with paper muffin liners.

Putting the muffins together

In a large bowl, mix together the flour, cornmeal, sugar, baking powder, and baking soda. Add the egg substitute, buttermilk, and vegetable oil and stir just until blended.

For breakfast or dinner tonight

Preheat the oven to 350°F. Pour the batter into the prepared muffin tins. Bake for 30 minutes or until a toothpick inserted in the center of a muffin comes out clean and the muffins are golden brown.

To freeze

Pour the batter into the prepared muffin pans and cover the entire pan with plastic wrap. Freeze in the muffin pan. When the muffins are completely frozen, remove from the pan and place in a resealable freezer bag. Label, date, and freeze for up to 3 months.

Return the frozen muffins to a muffin pan and bake in a preheated 350°F oven for 35 to 45 minutes, until a toothpick inserted in the center of the muffin comes out clean and the muffins are golden brown.

Baked Shoestring Potatoes

We don't know anyone—babies, finicky teenagers, grandparents—who doesn't LOVE potatoes made this way. We use frozen potatoes in the shoestring size but you can use whatever frozen potatoes you like best for this dish. Adding the ham can make it a part of wonderful comfort dinner.

Serves 6

For One	For Three	Ingredients
1	3	28-ounce bag(s) frozen shoestring potatoes
1 pound	3 pounds	nonfat sour cream
2 tablespoons	6 tablespoons	low-fat yogurt-based spread or butter
1	3	10-ounce can(s) cream of chicken soup
2 cups (12 ounces)	6 cups (2 pounds)	ham, diced, optional
1 cup (4 ounces)	3 cups (12 ounces)	low-fat shredded cheese blend (see page 34)

Putting the dish together

In a large bowl, combine the potatoes, sour cream, spread, soup, ham, if desired, and cheese. Mix to combine. Pour into a 9 × 13-inch baking dish, or if you are preparing a triple batch, divide equally among the three dishes. Sprinkle each with 1 cup of the cheese.

For dinner tonight

Preheat the oven to 375°F. Bake, uncovered, for approximately 45 minutes, until the cheese is melted and bubbly and the potatoes are cooked through.

To freeze

Cover with plastic wrap and heavy-duty aluminum foil. Label, date, and freeze for up to 3 months. Thaw at room temperature before cooking as directed above.

Use your slow cooker to cook your dinners. This is a great way to take dinner right from the freezer in the morning and come home to the aroma of a dinner already cooked.

PASTA

Chances are, pasta, whether spaghetti, linguine, penne, rotini, or any one of dozens of shapes and strands tossed in a sauce of tomatoes, pesto, cheese, olive oil, and garlic, or just a pat of yogurt-based spread or butter—shows up on your dinner table at least once each week. It's not surprising, given the chameleon-like nature of these noodles. With the twist of the lid on a jar of sun-dried tomatoes or artichokes in olive oil, for example, you can turn plain pasta into a delicious dinner. When the occasion calls for a pasta dish that appears to have been lovingly tended to rather than tossed together, turn to the recipes in this chapter. While it includes the baked pasta dishes everyone knows and loves—Tried-and-True Lasagne (page 128), Baked Ziti (page 126), and Manicotti (page 120)—there are many others, all of which, like these classics, feature pasta baked in a sauce. Tuna Tortellini Gratin (page 122), Penne with Rosemary Chicken (page 116), and My Big Dream Greek Pasta (page 108) are just a few of the favorites that are regularly requested in our homes. Nothing brings us more pleasure—and less anxiety about what to have for dinner—than having one of these dishes in the freezer. Baked pastas are among the easiest dishes to freeze—there's no assembly on the night you decide to serve them and they taste as fresh as, or better, than the day they were prepared. What's more, they can go straight from freezer to oven to table.

My Big Dream Greek Pasta

If you've never seen *My Big Fat Greek Wedding,* rent it and serve this for an evening filled with laughter and good food. We also like to bring this flavorful pasta and a copy of the movie to friends who need a bit of humor in their lives.

Serves 6

For One	For Three	Ingredient
		nonstick cooking spray
1 pound	3 pounds	rigatoni
1	3	zucchini, sliced into ½-inch rounds
1	3	15-ounce can(s) diced tomatoes with juice
1 tablespoon	3 tablespoons	minced garlic
1	3	red onion(s), diced
1½ pounds	4½ pounds	cooked boneless, skinless chicken breasts, diced
2 tablespoons	¼ cup plus 2 tablespoons	olive oil
1 cup (4 ounces)	3 cups (12 ounces)	crumbled feta cheese
1 teaspoon	1 tablespoon	grated lemon zest
2 teaspoons	2 tablespoons	dried oregano
1 teaspoon	3 teaspoons	Italian seasoning

For One	For Three	Ingredient
½ teaspoon	1½ teaspoons	kosher salt
½ teaspoon	1½ teaspoons	black pepper
1 cup (4 ounces)	3 cups (12 ounces)	grated Parmesan cheese
1 cup (4 ounces)	3 cups (12 ounces)	shredded mozzarella cheese

Spray one (three) 9 × 13-inch baking dish(es) with nonstick cooking spray.

Putting the pasta together

Bring a large pot of water to a boil. Add the pasta and cook just until tender, 3 to 5 minutes. Drain and place in the prepared baking dish(es), dividing the pasta equally among the three dishes if you are preparing a triple batch. In a large bowl, combine the zucchini, tomatoes, garlic, onion(s), chicken, olive oil, feta, lemon zest, oregano, Italian seasoning, salt, and pepper and mix until incorporated. Spoon the mixture over the pasta, dividing it equally among the three dishes if you are preparing a triple batch. Sprinkle with the Parmesan and mozzarella.

If you plan to freeze cooked pasta dishes, do not fully cook the pasta. It should be a bit chewier than al dente.

For dinner tonight

Preheat the oven to 350°F. Cover with aluminum foil and bake for 45 minutes. Remove the foil and bake for 10 minutes more or until the top is golden and the cheese is bubbly.

To freeze

Cover with plastic wrap and heavy-duty aluminum foil. Label, date, and freeze for up to 3 months. Thaw at room temperature before cooking as directed above.

Baked Pesto Ravioli with Chicken

Ravioli is a staple found in the refrigerator or freezer section of most grocery stores. We use the cheese-filled variety here, but you can use any kind you like. Omit the cooked chicken, if desired. **Serves 6**

For One	For Three	Ingredient
		nonstick cooking spray
2 pounds	6 pounds	cheese-filled ravioli, fresh or frozen
1 pound	3 pounds	cooked chicken breasts in ½-inch slices
⅔ cup	2 cups	chicken broth
2 cups	6 cups	zucchini, cut into ½-inch rounds
½ cup	1½ cups	red bell pepper, chopped into ½-inch pieces
½ cup	1 cup	chopped scallions
½ cup	1½ cups	store-bought basil pesto sauce
½ teaspoon	1½ teaspoons	kosher salt
½ teaspoon	1½ teaspoons	black pepper
1 cup (4 ounces)	3 cups (12 ounces)	grated Parmesan cheese

Spray one (three) 9 × 13-inch baking dish(es) with nonstick cooking spray.

Putting the pasta together

Combine the ravioli, chicken, chicken broth, zucchini, bell pepper, scallions, pesto, salt, pepper, and Parmesan in a large bowl. Stir gently to mix the ingredients. If you are preparing a triple batch, divide the remainder equally between two resealable freezer bags.

For dinner tonight

Preheat the oven to 350°F. Cover the dish with aluminum foil and bake for 1 hour or until bubbly.

To freeze

Label, date, and freeze for up to 3 months. Thaw at room temperature before baking as directed above.

Fettuccine with Chicken and Asparagus

The addition of Dijon mustard gives this satisfying spring pasta a nice kick. The pasta will cook to a firm, toothsome texture as it bakes in the sauce; if you want softer noodles, cook the dish a bit longer. **Serves 6**

For One	For Three	Ingredients
		nonstick cooking spray
¾ pound	2¼ pounds	fettuccine, cooked
⅔ pound 1½ cups, chopped	2 pounds 4½ cups, chopped	asparagus, cut into 2-inch pieces
1½ pounds	4½ pounds	cooked chicken breasts in ½-inch slices
1 cup (4 ounces)	3 cups (12 ounces)	sliced mushrooms
½ cup	1½ cups	yellow onion, diced
zest of 1	zest of 3	lemon(s), grated
1 teaspoon	3 teaspoons	kosher salt
½ teaspoon	1½ teaspoons	black pepper
2 cups	6 cups	nonfat milk
¼ cup	¾ cups	white wine
½ cup	1½ cups	Alfredo sauce
½ cup	1½ cups	Dijon mustard

Spray one (three) 9 × 13-inch baking dish(es) with nonstick cooking spray.

Putting the pasta together

Combine the fettuccine, asparagus, chicken, mushrooms, onion, lemon zest, salt, and pepper in a large bowl. Set aside. Combine the milk, wine, Alfredo sauce, and Dijon mustard in another bowl, mixing until smooth. Add to the chicken and pasta mixture and toss to coat thoroughly. Pour the mixture into the baking dish. If you are preparing a triple batch, divide the remaining mixture equally between two resealable freezer bags.

For dinner tonight

Preheat the oven to 350°F. Cover the baking dish with aluminum foil and bake for 45 minutes or until the pasta is tender and the surface is bubbly.

To freeze

Label, date, and freeze for up to 3 months. Thaw before cooking as directed above.

Wash your lemons, limes, and oranges before zesting the rind. Avoid the white part or pith of the fruit as it is bitter.

Baked Pasta and Lemon Chicken

This is the ultimate pantry dinner; you're likely to have all of the ingredients on hand to make at least a single batch. If you have a seafood craving, simply substitute the same amount of canned minced clams or shrimp for the cooked chicken.

Serves 6

For One	For Three	Ingredients
		nonstick cooking spray
4 cups (6 ounces)	12 cups (18 ounces)	cooked spaghetti
1½ pounds	4½ pounds	cooked chicken, diced
½ cup	1½ cup	fresh parsley, chopped
2½ teaspoons	2 tablespoons plus 1½ teaspoons	minced garlic
2 teaspoons	2 tablespoons	grated lemon zest
1½ teaspoons	1 tablespoon plus 1½ teaspoons	dried marjoram
1 teaspoon	1 tablespoon	kosher salt
½ teaspoon	1½ teaspoons	black pepper
¼ teaspoon	¾ teaspoon	red pepper flakes
⅔ cup	2 cups	white wine
½ cup	1½ cups	chicken broth

For One	For Three	Ingredients
¼ cup	**¾ cup**	**olive oil**
2 tablespoons	**¼ cup**	**lemon juice**

Spray one (three) 9 × 13-inch baking dish(es) with nonstick cooking spray.

Putting the pasta together

In a large bowl, combine the ingredients and stir to combine. Transfer the mixture to a resealable freezer bag, dividing it equally among three if you are preparing a triple batch. Seal the bags tightly and place one bag in the refrigerator until you are ready to cook dinner.

For dinner tonight

Preheat the oven to 350°F. Transfer the chicken and pasta mixture from the bag into the prepared baking dish. Cover with aluminum foil and bake for 45 minutes or until the chicken is cooked through. Alternatively, spray a large skillet with nonstick cooking spray and heat over medium-high heat. Cook the chicken and pasta mixture for 15 to 20 minutes until the chicken is cooked through.

If using lemon juice when freezing a recipe, bottled juice is easier and just as good as fresh.

To freeze

Label, date, and freeze for up to 3 months. Thaw in the refrigerator before cooking as directed above.

Penne with Rosemary Chicken

The pasta will cook al dente as it bakes in the sauce, so there's no need to boil the pasta first. If you prefer a softer noodle, bake the dish a bit longer. Let this dish cool before serving to allow the sauce to thicken.

Serves 6

For One	For Three	Ingredients
		nonstick cooking spray
1 pound	3 pounds	diced cooked chicken
1 pound	3 pounds	penne pasta
1 cup (4 ounces)	3 cups (12 ounces)	low-fat shredded cheese blend (see page 34)
½ cup	1½ cups	yellow onion(s), diced
2 tablespoons	¼ cup plus 2 tablespoons	chopped pimentos, drained
1 tablespoon	3 tablespoons	dried rosemary
1 teaspoon	1 tablespoon	kosher salt
½ teaspoon	1½ teaspoons	black pepper
2 cups	6 cups	nonfat milk
1½	4½	15-ounce can(s) cream of mushroom soup

Spray one (three) 9 × 13-inch baking dish(es) with nonstick cooking spray.

Putting the pasta together

Place all the ingredients into a large bowl and stir to combine. Transfer the mixture to a resealable freezer bag, dividing it equally among three bags if you are preparing a triple batch.

For dinner tonight

Preheat the oven to 350°F. Place the contents of a bag into the prepared baking dish and cover with foil. Bake for 1 to 1¼ hours. Or, place in a crockpot, set on low heat, and cook for 5 to 6 hours.

To freeze

Label, date, and freeze for up to 3 months. Thaw in the refrigerator before cooking as directed above.

Think Outside the Foil Pan

Although you may assemble your dinners in foil pans, that doesn't mean you have to serve them from the foil pans.

Spice It Up: Peel away the foil while your dinner is frozen. Place in a sprayed baking dish, thaw, and bake. The glass baking dish dresses up your entrée and emphasizes the fact that it's homemade.

Family Style: Transfer the fully cooked entrée to a family-sized serving platter. The serving platter adds grace and style to an everyday dinner.

Elegant Entertaining: If you're hosting a dinner party or feeding an extra-large family, assemble two dinners. Bake them in foil pans, spoon the contents of both dishes onto a beautiful serving tray, and add a garnish. Serves 12 to 15 people easily!

Summer Pasta

Make this at the height of summer when tomatoes and basil are at their peak flavor. For a vegetarian alternative or to serve as a side dish, omit the sausage.

Serves 6

For One	For Three	Ingredients
		nonstick cooking spray
1 pound	3 pounds	cooked sweet Italian sausage, cut into 1-inch pieces
2 cups (8 ounces)	6 cups (1½ pounds)	mozzarella cheese in ½-inch cubes
8 ounces	1½ pounds	plum tomatoes, diced
¼ cup	¾ cup	olive oil
1 cup	3 cups	chopped fresh basil
1 teaspoon	1 tablespoon	kosher salt
1 teaspoon	1 tablespoon	black pepper
1 pound	3 pounds	penne

Spray one (three) 9 × 13-inch baking dish(es) with nonstick cooking spray.

Putting the pasta together

Combine all of the ingredients except the pasta in a large bowl. If you are preparing a triple batch, divide the remaining mixture equally between two resealable freezer bags.

For dinner tonight

Heat a large pot of water to boiling. Add the pasta and stir. Cook the pasta just until tender, 5 to 8 minutes. Drain the pasta and toss with the ingredients in the bowl until the cheese is soft, about 3 minutes. Serve immediately. Hot pasta is the trick; it will heat all the other ingredients just enough to wilt the basil and soften the cheese.

To freeze

Drain the pasta and rinse with cold water. Toss the pasta with the ingredients in the resealable freezer bags. Label, date, and freeze for up to 3 months. Thaw before baking. Transfer to the prepared baking dish. Cover with aluminum foil and bake in a 350°F oven for 20 minutes or until thoroughly heated and the mozzarella is soft and just starting to melt.

"Teens who have family dinners five or more times a week are twice as likely to get A's in school compared to those who have family dinners twice a week or less."

—The National Center on Addiction and Substance Abuse (CASA) at Columbia University

Manicotti

You don't need a pastry piping bag to fill the manicotti; just spoon the filling into a 1-gallon resealable bag, seal it, snip away one corner, and squeeze the filling through. Or, you may simply use a spoon. **Serves 6**

For One	For Three	Ingredients
		nonstick cooking spray
3 cups	9 cups	store-bought marinara sauce
2 cups (1 pound)	6 cups (3 pounds)	nonfat cottage cheese
1 cup (4 ounces)	3 cups (12 ounces)	shredded skim mozzarella cheese
½ cup (2 ounces)	1½ cups (6 ounces)	grated Parmesan cheese
½ cup	1½ cups	nonfat egg substitute
1 teaspoon	1 tablespoon	dried oregano
1 teaspoon	1 tablespoon	dried basil
1 teaspoon	1 tablespoon	kosher salt
½ teaspoon	1½ teaspoons	black pepper
12	36	manicotti shells

Spray one (three) 9 × 13-inch baking dish(es) with nonstick cooking spray.

Putting the pasta together

Spread 1 cup of the marinara sauce on the bottom of the prepared baking dish(es). Set aside. In a large bowl, combine all the ingredients except the manicotti and stir until incorporated. Spoon (or use a resealable plastic bag to make a piping bag and squeeze) the cheese mixture into the shells, dividing it equally among them, and place the filled shells over the sauce in the baking dish(es). Spread the remaining marinara sauce evenly over the top of the shells, dividing it equally if you are preparing a triple batch.

For dinner tonight

Preheat the oven to 350°F. Cover the dish with foil and bake for 45 minutes to 1 hour, until the sauce is bubbly.

To freeze

Cover with plastic wrap and foil. Label, date, and freeze for up to 3 months. Thaw before cooking as directed above.

Let's Talk

Choose a dinner theme.

Turn the dining room into an Italian restaurant. Use a red-and-white-checkered tablecloth and light the room with candles in Chianti bottles.

If tacos are on the menu, fill it out with all things Mexican, and play appropriate music, too.

Other themes: Hawaiian luau, red foods on Valentine's Day, green foods on Saint Patrick's Day, winter picnics, breakfast for dinner, hobo packet dinners.

Tuna Tortellini Gratin

This is not your mother's tuna noodle casserole! This dinner, though reminiscent of old-fashioned comfort food, is filled with delicious surprises. Purchase the tortellini at your grocery store fresh from the refrigerated section. If you use fresh tortellini, there's no need to precook it. We like to use a sweet white wine and albacore tuna packed in water for this dish.

Serves 6

For One	For Three	Ingredients
		nonstick cooking spray
1¼ pounds	3¾ pounds	cooked, fresh cheese-filled tortellini
2	8	6-ounce can(s) albacore tuna in water, drained
½ cup	1 cup	red bell pepper, chopped
½ cup	1 cup	onion, diced
1	3	10.5-ounce jar(s) store-bought Alfredo sauce
½ cup	1½ cups	white wine
1 teaspoon	1 tablespoon	kosher salt
½ teaspoon	1½ teaspoons	black pepper
1 cup	3 cups	seasoned bread crumbs
3 tablespoons	½ cup plus 1 tablespoon	olive oil

Spray one (three) 9 × 13-inch baking dish(es) with nonstick cooking spray.

Putting the pasta together

In a large bowl, combine all the ingredients except the bread crumbs and olive oil and stir. Transfer the mixture to the prepared baking dish(es), dividing it equally among the three dishes if you are preparing a triple batch. Sprinkle bread crumbs over the top of each baking dish and drizzle with olive oil.

For dinner tonight

Preheat the oven to 350°F. Cover the dish with aluminum foil and bake for 45 minutes to 1 hour, until bubbly. Remove the foil and slide the dish under the broiler for 3 to 4 minutes, until the topping is golden brown.

To freeze

Cover the dishes with plastic wrap and aluminum foil. Label, date, and freeze for up to 3 months. Thaw at room temperature before cooking as directed above.

Dream Macaroni and Cheese

Good old American cheese and pasta bakes up with a crisp seasoned topping. This is old-fashioned flavor that freezes beautifully. **Serves 6**

For One	For Three	Ingredients
2 cups	6 cups	dry macaroni pasta
3 tablespoons	9 tablespoons	low-fat yogurt-based spread or butter
2 tablespoons	6 tablespoons	all-purpose flour
1 dash	3 dashes	hot chili pepper sauce
1 teaspoon	3 teaspoons	kosher salt
2 cups	6 cups	nonfat milk
2 cups	6 cups	American cheese, cubed
1 cup	3 cups	seasoned bread crumbs

Spray one (three) 9 × 13-inch baking dish(es) with nonstick cooking spray.

Putting your dinner together

Cook the macaroni according to the package directions. On the stovetop over medium heat, melt the butter in a large skillet. Blend in the flour until golden brown, about 5 minutes. Season with the hot sauce and salt. Pour in the milk and simmer until thickened and bubbly. Add the cheese cubes and stir until melted. Add the macaroni and stir until combined.

Pour the mixture into the prepared baking dish(es), dividing equally among the three dishes if you are preparing a triple batch, and sprinkle with the seasoned bread crumbs.

For dinner tonight

Bake in a 325°F oven, uncovered, for 1 hour or until a knife comes out clean when inserted.

To freeze

Label, date, and freeze for up to 3 months. Thaw before cooking as directed above.

Getting Them to the Table

How to get your family to the dinner table—without raising your voice:

- Play a family theme song and by the time the song is over, everyone knows they should be at the table.
- Whoever gets to the table first:
    - Sits in a special seat.
    - Asks the first question at the dinner table.
    - Gets to pick what to have for dinner the next night.
    - Gets a star on a chart. The family member with the most stars at the end of the month chooses what the family outing will be. Adults can be on the chart, too.

Baked Ziti

This is an excellent dish to make for a crowd, especially during the cold-weather months. It's the ultimate comfort food—hearty, heartwarming, and familiar.

Serves 6

For One	For Three	Ingredients
		nonstick cooking spray
1 pound	3 pounds	ziti
1 teaspoon	1 tablespoon	dried rosemary
1 teaspoon	1 tablespoon	Italian seasoning
½ cup	1½ cups	nonfat sour cream
½ cup (4 ounces)	1½ cups (12 ounces)	nonfat cottage cheese
3 cups	9 cups	store-bought marinara sauce
1 pound	3 pounds	extra lean ground beef
1 cup	3 cups	yellow onion(s), chopped
4 teaspoons	¼ cup	minced garlic
3 slices (3 ounces)	9 slices (8 ounces)	provolone cheese
1 cup (4 ounces)	3 cups (12 ounces)	shredded skim mozzarella cheese

Spray one (three) 9 × 13-inch baking dish(es) with nonstick cooking spray.

Putting the pasta together

Add the pasta to a large pot of boiling water. Boil until just tender, about 3 minutes. Drain and transfer to a large bowl. Add the rosemary, Italian seasoning, sour cream, cottage cheese, and marinara sauce and stir until incorporated. Transfer the pasta mixture to the prepared baking dish(es), dividing it equally among the three dishes if you are preparing a triple batch. Spray a large skillet with nonstick cooking spray and heat over medium-high heat. Add the ground beef, onion(s), and garlic and cook until browned, about 10 minutes. Drain off any excess fat. Sprinkle the ground beef mixture over the pasta, dividing it equally among the three dishes if you are preparing a triple batch. Top with the provolone and mozzarella.

Have a family meeting and look at the recipes together. Let each child choose one that sounds promising. Allow your children to help prepare the salad, vegetables, or bread.

For dinner tonight

Preheat the oven to 350°F. Cover the dish with aluminum foil sprayed with nonstick cooking spray and bake for 45 minutes. Remove the foil and bake until browned and bubbly, about 10 minutes more.

To freeze

Cover the dishes with plastic wrap and foil. Label, date, and freeze for up to 3 months. Thaw at room temperature before baking as directed above.

Tried-and-True Lasagne

Lasagne noodles can be layered with just about any filling, but we love the flavors of the classic tomato, cheese, and herb combinations. There's never a more welcome dish on the table than a bubbling, piping, hot lasagne, so make it in multiples to have on hand when the craving strikes.

Serves 6

For One	For Three	Ingredients
		nonstick cooking spray
1 pound	3 pounds	extra lean ground beef
2 cups	6 cups	store-bought marinara sauce
1	3	15-ounce can(s) diced roasted tomatoes, drained
1 cup	3 cups	roasted red peppers, diced
¼ cup	¾ cup	tomato paste
2 teaspoons	6 tablespoons	minced garlic
2 tablespoons	¼ cup plus 2 tablespoons	dried parsley
1 tablespoon	3 tablespoons	Italian seasoning
1 tablespoon	3 tablespoons	dried basil
1 tablespoon	3 tablespoons	sugar
¼ cup	¾ cup	nonfat egg substitute

For One	For Three	Ingredients
1 cup (8 ounces)	3 cups (1½ pounds)	nonfat cottage cheese
1 cup (4 ounces)	3 cups (12 ounces)	grated Parmesan cheese
¾ cup (6 ounces)	2¼ cups (1 pound, 2 ounces)	part skim ricotta cheese
1 teaspoon	1 tablespoon	kosher salt
½ teaspoon	1½ teaspoons	black pepper
8	24	lasagne noodles
2 cups (8 ounces)	6 cups (1½ pounds)	shredded skim mozzarella cheese

Spray one (three) 9 × 13-inch baking dish(es) with nonstick cooking spray.

Putting the pasta together

Heat a large skillet over medium-high heat. Put in the ground beef and cook until browned, about 10 minutes. Drain off any excess fat. In a large bowl, combine the cooked ground beef, marinara sauce, tomatoes, roasted peppers, tomato paste, garlic, parsley, Italian seasoning, basil, and sugar and stir until incorporated. In a separate bowl, combine the egg substitute, cottage cheese, Parmesan, ricotta, salt, and pepper and stir until incorporated. Layer the mixtures into the prepared baking dish(es) in the following order: ½ cup of the sauce mixture, 4 lasagna noodles, 1½ cups of the cheese mixture, and 1 cup of mozzarella cheese. Repeat, beginning with the noodles and ending with the cheese.

If you need more pans, line your baking pan with foil, build your casserole, and freeze it. Remove the frozen casserole from the pan, wrap it with another layer of foil, and place it back into the freezer without the pan. When ready to thaw and bake, unwrap the foil, and place the dinner back into the original baking dish.

For dinner tonight

Preheat the oven to 375°F. Cover the dish with aluminum foil sprayed with nonstick cooking spray and bake for 20 minutes. Remove the foil and bake for 15 minutes more, until the cheese is melted.

To freeze

Cover with plastic wrap and aluminum foil. Label, date, and freeze for up to 3 months. Thaw at room temperature before cooking as directed above.

Let's Talk

Set the mood for a comfortable, relaxing meal. Get the conversation going as soon as everyone is seated by asking each person a question relevant only to him or her.

Ask about specific people who are important in your family members' lives.

Ask everyone to tell you three things about their day that you might not otherwise have known.

Compliment the cook and ask how the dinner was prepared.

Discuss after-dinner plans or plans for the next day.

To keep your children around the dinner table ask open-ended questions. Who did you see today? Invite them to do something with you after dinnertime.

Get Your Children Involved

Encouraging your children to make healthy food choices and to become interested in mealtimes can be difficult. There are a few ideas we've found to be successful in inspiring participation in mealtimes from our own children.

Here are some ideas to help get your children involved in Dream Dinners:

Have a family meeting and talk about dinner options. Let each child choose one that he or she would like.

Modify recipes to suit your family's tastes—lighten up on onions or garlic or spices or add more of an ingredient they like. Use ingredients that your children might not like in only half the dish. Point out that you made the other half specially for them.

For children seven years or older, invite them to make their own sandwiches and bring them to the table to eat with the rest of the family. After a while, they will get tired of that and want to eat what everyone else is eating.

Encourage children to help you prepare the dinners in triple-batch form, assembly-line style.

Begin the month with their favorite dishes. Once they're hooked, expand their taste buds with new foods and flavors.

Encourage your children to take a "No thank-you bite," in an effort to get them to at least try the meal. If they don't like it, instruct them to say, "No thank you."

Baked Spaghetti

A Dream Dinners favorite always voted to be on the "best of the best" menu—spaghetti and meatballs baked casserole style. There's no last-minute draining of noodles and plating with the sauce—just pull the casserole from the oven and bring it to the table. **Serves 6**

For One	For Three	Ingredients
		nonstick cooking spray
1 cup	3 cups	yellow onion(s), diced
1 teaspoon	1 tablespoon	minced garlic
½	1½	green bell pepper(s), chopped
2	6	15-ounce can(s) diced tomatoes, with juice
1 cup (4 ounces)	3 cups (12 ounces)	mushrooms, sliced
1 teaspoon	1 tablespoon	dried basil
1 tablespoon	3 tablespoons	dried oregano
1 teaspoon	1 tablespoon	kosher salt
½ teaspoon	1½ teaspoons	black pepper
6 ounces	18 ounces	spaghetti
1	3	16-ounce bag(s) frozen meatballs
1 cup (4 ounces)	3 cups (12 ounces)	grated Parmesan cheese

For One	For Three	Ingredients
2 cups (8 ounces)	6 cups ($1\frac{1}{2}$ pounds)	**low-fat shredded cheese blend (see page 34)**
1	3	**10-ounce can(s) cream of mushroom soup**
1	3	**2.4-ounce can(s) sliced black olives, drained**

Spray one (three) 9 × 13-inch baking dish(es) with nonstick cooking spray.

Putting the pasta together

Cook the spaghetti according to the package directions.

Combine the onion(s), garlic, pepper(s), tomatoes, mushrooms, basil, oregano, salt, and pepper in a bowl and stir until incorporated. Set aside. Place half of the cooked spaghetti in the bottom of the prepared baking dish(es). Layer 6 meatballs and half of the vegetable mixture over the spaghetti in the baking dish(es). Sprinkle with half of the Parmesan and half of the shredded cheese. Repeat, beginning with the remaining spaghetti and ending with the vegetable mixture. Set aside. In a bowl, combine the mushroom soup with an equal amount of water and pour over the baking dish(es). Sprinkle with the remaining Parmesan, shredded cheese, and olives, dividing equally among the three dishes if you are preparing a triple batch.

For dinner tonight

Preheat the oven to 350°F. Cover with aluminum foil and bake for 1 hour. Remove the foil and bake for 30 minutes more.

To freeze

Cover with plastic wrap and foil. Label, date, and freeze for up to 3 months. Thaw at room temperature before cooking as directed above.

DINNERS

If you're like most busy people, you've got dinnertime down to a science. And for most of us, that means relying on the same five foolproof dishes in our recipe repertoire week in and week out, without much variation. If you changed the menu lineup much at all, it might mean unexpected trips to the grocery store, unplanned preparation time, and a last-minute discovery that you're out of an essential spice. But imagine if you could revise those five staple dishes and expand your choices to include dozens of delicious dinners—all of which require little after-work effort to get on the table. This chapter includes dozens of just such dishes; they call for common pantry ingredients, basic techniques and equipment, and just a few bowls, pots, and pans. What's more, every single one freezes beautifully. Why resort to a repetitive menu when you can just as easily make Provençal Flank Steak (page 140), Spicy Lime Chicken (page 186), and Seafood Cioppino (page 72)? Round out the week with Beef and Corn Enchiladas (page 154) and succulent Mango Curry Chicken (page 190). If you've prepared these dishes the Dream Dinners way—by making three entrées instead of one—you'll have ten more nights' worth of satisfying, healthy meals to choose from.

Asian Steak

If you have been looking for the perfect marinade for steak, look no further. This mix of hoisin sauce, honey, and sesame oil imparts a beautiful lacquer and rich flavor to the meat. Do not worry if the marinade does not freeze completely; it will still taste as if you made it the day you served it.

Serves 6

For One	For Three	Ingredients
6	18	4-ounce top sirloin steaks
½ cup	1½ cups	hoisin sauce
¼ cup	¾ cup	honey
¼ cup	¾ cup	sesame oil
¼ cup	¾ cup	lite soy sauce
¼ cup	¾ cup	white wine
¼ cup	¾ cup	sesame seeds
1 teaspoon	1 tablespoon	minced garlic

Putting the dinner together

Combine the ingredients in a resealable freezer bag and seal it, dividing equally among the three bags if you are preparing a triple batch. Gently knead the bag to mix the ingredients. Place the bag into a second resealable freezer bag and seal it tightly.

For dinner tonight

Marinate the steaks in the refrigerator for at least 1 hour. Prepare a hot grill. Grill the steaks for 3 minutes per side, or until the internal temperature reaches 100°F for rare, 130°F for medium-rare, or 165°F for well done. Alternatively, heat a nonstick skillet over high heat. Add the steaks and sear for 3 minutes on each side. Remove the steaks from the heat. Meanwhile, boil the marinade for 5 minutes and drizzle it over the top of the steaks.

We always use lite soy sauce, which reduces the sodium content by 40 percent.

To freeze

Label, date, and freeze for up to 3 months. Thaw before cooking as directed above.

Pepper Steak

This is wonderful served warm over rice or with a baked potato, or served at room temperature over chopped romaine for lunch. You can use red bell peppers or a combination of green, yellow, orange, and red bell peppers for a colorful alternative. Freezing the meat for 30 minutes makes it easy to cut into thin, even slices. Using your crockpot will have you coming home to the delicious smell of dinner.

Serves 6

For One	For Three	Ingredients
1½ pounds	4½ to 5 pounds	beef bottom round, ½-inch slices cut across grain
2 cups	6 cups	green peppers, cut into ½-inch-thick slices
1 cup	3 cups	onion(s), chopped
1	3	15-ounce can(s) diced tomatoes with juice
1 teaspoon	1 tablespoon	minced garlic
¼ cup	¾ cup	Worcestershire sauce
1 tablespoon	3 tablespoons	cornstarch
1 tablespoon	3 tablespoons	sugar
½ teaspoon	1½ teaspoons	kosher salt
½ teaspoon	1½ teaspoons	black pepper

Putting the dinner together

In a large bowl, combine the ingredients and add ½ cup water to the bowl and stir, or add ½ cup to each of three bowls if you are preparing a triple batch. Reserve one batch for dinner tonight; place the remaining two portions into resealable freezer bags.

For dinner tonight

Pour the mixture into a crockpot set on low. Cook for 6 to 8 hours on the low setting.

To freeze

Label, date, and freeze for up to 3 months. Thaw in the refrigerator before cooking as directed above.

Successful Crockpot Cooking

Some slow cookers run hotter than others, so here are some guidelines for comparable cooking times.

Conventional Recipe Baked in the Oven at 350°F	Slow Cooker Low (200°F)	Slow Cooker High (300°F)
15–30 minutes	4–6 hours	1½–2 hours
35–45 minutes	6–10 hours	3–4 hours
50 mins–3 hours	8–18 hours	4–6 hours

Provençal Flank Steak

Many cuts of meat, especially flank steak, benefit from marinating. After cooking, let the steak rest for 5 minutes before slicing it thinly across the grain. This allows all of the flavorful juices to remain in the meat, making it the most succulent it can be.

Serves 6

For One	For Three	Ingredients
1 tablespoon	3 tablespoons	minced garlic
1 teaspoon	1 tablespoon	dried rosemary
½ teaspoon	1½ teaspoons	chili powder
½ teaspoon	1½ teaspoons	paprika
½ teaspoon	1½ teaspoons	black pepper
½ cup	1½ cups	honey
1 cup	3 cups	soy sauce
½ cup	1½ cups	red wine
1½ pounds	4½ pounds	flank steak

Putting the dinner together

In a large bowl, combine all the ingredients except the steak. Pour the marinade into a resealable freezer bag, dividing it equally among three bags if you are preparing a triple batch. Place 1½ pounds of flank steak into the bag(s).

For dinner tomorrow night

Marinate the steak in the refrigerator overnight. Preheat the broiler or prepare a hot grill. Remove the steak from the marinade and sear on both sides, about 5 minutes per side. Meanwhile, pour the marinade into a saucepan and boil over high heat for 5 minutes. Slice the flank steak into paper-thin slices across the grain. Drizzle the marinade over the steak and serve.

Red meats and thick cut fish may be cooked using the muscle between your thumb and forefinger as a guide. Make a fist and squeeze hard. Press on that muscle and note the resistance. Well-done meat and fish will feel the same when pressed. Cooking to medium will feel the same to the touch as a light fist, while rare will feel the same as a relaxed fist.

To freeze

Label, date, and freeze for up to 3 months. Thaw in the refrigerator before cooking as directed above.

Slow-Cooked Barbecued Beef

This is a wonderful dish to eat outdoors on those late summer nights when there's a hint of fall in the air. Serve on burger buns for a simple, filling meal. Pull it out of your freezer and your crockpot does all the work. This is also great when served over baked potatoes. **Serves 6**

For One	For Three	Ingredients
2 pounds	6 pounds	beef chuck roast, fat trimmed
1 cup	3 cups	yellow onion(s), diced
1 teaspoon	1 tablespoon	minced garlic
2 cups	6 cups	ketchup
¼ cup	¾ cup	balsamic vinegar
2 tablespoons	¼ cup plus 2 tablespoons	Dijon mustard
¼ cup	¾ cup	packed brown sugar
2 tablespoons	¼ cup plus 2 tablespoons	Worcestershire sauce
2 teaspoon	2 tablespoons	liquid smoke flavoring
1 teaspoon	1 tablespoon	kosher salt
1 teaspoon	1 tablespoon	black pepper

Putting the dinner together

Place the roast in a crockpot. If you are preparing a triple batch, place the remaining roasts in each of two resealable freezer bags.

In a large bowl, combine the remaining ingredients and mix well. If you are preparing a triple batch, pour equal amounts over the three roasts.

For dinner tonight

Cook the roast in the crockpot on the low setting for 6 to 8 hours, until the meat falls apart easily. Shred the meat with a fork and serve over hamburger buns or baked potatoes.

To freeze

Label, date, and freeze for up to 3 months. Thaw in the refrigerator before cooking as directed above.

"Parents' table talk can help children to understand their families. . . . Positive family mealtime conversations can . . . foster positive relationships that help children and parents talk through tough issues when they arise."

—Dr. Karen Cullen, Baylor College of Medicine

Beef Stir-Fry

This dish is the one that might just entice your children to eat their vegetables. The baby corn seems to intrigue them the most. Look for the leanest cut of beef you can find, and trim off any excess fat before slicing. Freezing the meat for 30 minutes before you slice it makes it easy to cut into thin, even slices. Serve over linguine, rice noodles, or rice. **Serves 6**

For One	For Three	Ingredients
½ cup	1½ cups	soy sauce
3 tablespoons	½ cup plus 1 tablespoon	minced ginger
1 teaspoon	1 tablespoon	black pepper
½ teaspoon	1½ teaspoons	red pepper flakes
¼ cup	¾ cup	peanut butter
1 tablespoon	3 tablespoons	light brown sugar, packed
1 pound	3 pounds	beef bottom round, cut into ¼-inch-thick slices across the grain
4	12	celery, cut into ¾-inch pieces
1	3	carrot(s), sliced
1	3	15-ounce can(s) baby corn, drained
1	3	onion(s), thinly sliced

Putting the dinner together

In a large bowl, combine the soy sauce, ginger, black pepper, red pepper flakes, peanut butter, and brown sugar and stir to incorporate. Add the beef and toss to coat. Place the celery, carrot(s), corn, and onion(s) into a separate bag.

For dinner tonight

Heat a skillet over high heat. Add the meat and marinade mixture and cook just until the edges of the steak are browned, about 2 minutes. Add the vegetables and cook for 2 more minutes or until the vegetables are firm to the bite. Serve.

To freeze

Divide the remaining meat marinade mixture equally between two resealable freezer bags and seal. Divide the remaining mixed vegetables equally between two additional resealable freezer bags. Place one bag containing the meat marinade mixture into each of the vegetable bags. Label, date, and freeze for up to 3 months. Thaw in the refrigerator before cooking as directed above.

When stir-frying, hot pan-cold food is the rule. Heat the frying pan over high heat—if it's hot enough, a splash of water will dance on its surface—add the ingredients, stir-fry, and serve.

Sesame Marinated London Broil

Grilled London broil is the perfect summer dinner that will please a crowd. Make three and host a potluck where you serve the beef and everyone else brings the rest. You can have your butcher trim and cut this to the size you need.

Serves 6

For One	For Three	Ingredients
1	3	24-ounce London broil(s), fat trimmed
¼ cup	¾ cup	minced garlic
2 cups	6 cups	soy sauce
½ cup	1½ cups	scallions, chopped
¼ cup	¾ cup	sesame seeds
¼ teaspoon	¾ teaspoon	red pepper flakes
½ teaspoon	1½ teaspoons	black pepper
½ cup	1½ cups	rice vinegar
2 tablespoons	6 tablespoons	granulated sugar

Putting your dinner together

Place the London broil into a 1-gallon resealable freezer bag(s). Add each ingredient over the meat and seal tightly. Toss the bag to coat the London broil.

For dinner tonight

Marinate the meat in the refrigerator for at least 1 hour. Prepare a grill to medium-high. Grill the meat for 10 to 12 minutes per side, depending on the thickness. Alternatively, heat an oven broiler to high and spray a broiler pan with cooking spray. Place the meat on the sprayed pan and broil for 10 to 12 minutes per side, depending on the thickness. Let the meat rest for 5 minutes before slicing thinly across the grain. Meanwhile, boil the remaining marinade for 5 minutes on the stovetop and serve over the London broil.

To freeze

Label, date, and freeze for up to 3 months. Thaw before cooking as directed above.

Beef and Zucchini Casserole

Here is a great way to use an abundance of zucchini from the garden. Even better, give your neighbors this casserole rather than an armload of zucchini and they'll keep coming back for more! **Serves 6**

For One	For Three	Ingredients
		nonstick cooking spray
3 cups	9 cups	zucchini, cut into 1-inch rounds
1 cup	3 cups	yellow onion(s), diced
½ pound	1½ pounds	ground beef, browned and drained of any excess fat
1 teaspoon	1 tablespoon	minced garlic
1 teaspoon	1 tablespoon	dried basil
1 tablespoon	3 tablespoons	sugar
2 teaspoons	2 tablespoons	dried oregano
½ teaspoon	1½ teaspoons	garlic salt
½ teaspoon	1½ teaspoons	black pepper
1	3	28-ounce can(s) diced tomatoes with juice
1½ cups	4½ cups	seasoned dry stuffing mix
½ cup (2 ounces)	1½ cups (6 ounces)	grated Parmesan cheese
1 cup (4 ounces)	3 cups (12 ounces)	shredded part-skim mozzarella cheese

Spray one (three) 9 × 13-inch baking dish(es) with nonstick cooking spray.

Never dish up food for your children. Instead, let them serve themselves and ask for things to be passed to them. This way they learn to take responsibility for their choices and for the amounts taken.

Putting the dinner together

Layer the ingredients in the prepared baking dish(es) in the order listed.

For dinner tonight

Preheat the oven to 375°F. Bake uncovered for 1 hour or until the top is golden brown and the vegetables are fork tender.

To freeze

Cover with plastic wrap and heavy-duty aluminum foil. Label, date, and freeze for up to 3 months. Thaw in the refrigerator before cooking as directed above.

Citrus Marinated Beef Sirloin Steaks

Beef sirloin steaks will be tender and delicious after marinating in our tenderizing sauce.

Serves 6

For One	For Three	Ingredients
6	18	4-ounce top sirloin steaks
½ cup	1½ cups	orange juice concentrate, not diluted
½ cup	1½ cups	lime juice
½ cup	1½ cups	honey
2 tablespoons	6 tablespoons	olive oil
2 teaspoons	6 teaspoons	hot pepper sauce
2 tablespoons	6 tablespoons	minced garlic
1 tablespoons	3 tablespoons	ground cumin
1 teaspoon	3 teaspoons	black pepper

Putting your dinner together

Add the 6 steaks to a 1-gallon resealable freezer bag. Add each ingredient over the meat and seal tightly. Toss the bag to coat the steaks.

For dinner tonight

Marinate the meat in the refrigerator for at least 1 hour. Prepare a grill to high heat. Grill the meat for 5 minutes per side, depending on the thickness. Alternatively, heat an oven broiler to high and spray a broiler pan with cooking spray. Place the meat on the sprayed pan and broil for 5 minutes per side, depending on the thickness. Meanwhile, boil the remaining marinade for 5 minutes on the stovetop and serve over the steaks.

To freeze

Label, date, and freeze for up to 3 months. Thaw in the refrigerator before cooking as directed above.

Sloppy Joes

Sloppy Joanna, Sloppy Jonathan, Sloppy Johnny . . . whatever your child's name is, he or she will love this no-fuss, family-friendly dinner. There's no need to buy buns; the succulent meat is surrounded by a biscuit-like crust.

Serves 6

For One	For Three	Ingredients
		nonstick cooking spray
2 cups	6 cups	low-fat biscuit mix
⅔ cup	2 cups	low-fat buttermilk
¼ cup	¾ cup	nonfat egg substitute
1 pound	3 pounds	ground beef, cooked and drained of excess fat
1	3	1-ounce package(s) dry onion soup mix
1 cup	3 cups	store-bought marinara sauce
1 cup	3 cups	store-bought barbecue sauce
1 cup (4 ounces)	3 cups (12 ounces)	grated cheese blend (Cheddar, Monterey Jack, and mozzarella, see page 34)

Spray one (three) 9-inch pie plates with nonstick cooking spray.

Putting the dinner together

In a bowl, combine the biscuit mix, milk, and egg substitute and stir together until a soft ball forms. Press the dough into the bottom and up the sides of the pie plate, dividing it equally among three pie plates if you are preparing a triple batch.

In a separate large bowl, combine the ground beef, onion soup mix, and marinara and barbecue sauces and stir until thoroughly incorporated. Spread the mixture evenly over the dough in the pie plate, dividing the mixture equally among the three pie plates if you are preparing a triple batch. Sprinkle with the cheese.

For dinner tonight

Preheat the oven to 375°F. Bake the pie for approximately 45 minutes, until the cheese is melted and bubbly.

To freeze

Cover the pies with plastic wrap and heavy-duty aluminum foil. Label, date, and freeze for up to 3 months. Thaw in the refrigerator before cooking as directed above.

Beef and Corn Enchiladas

Serve these easy enchiladas with Spanish Rice and you have a quick weeknight dinner in an hour.

Serves 6

For One	For Three	Ingredients
		nonstick cooking spray
1 pound	3 pounds	extra lean ground beef
1	3	yellow onion(s), diced
2 teaspoons	2 tablespoons	minced garlic
1 cup	3 cups	nonfat sour cream
1	3	15-ounce can(s) diced tomatoes, drained
1 cup (8 ounces)	3 cups (1½ pounds)	low-fat ricotta cheese
1	3	7-ounce can(s) diced mild green chiles *or*
¼ cup	¾ cup	jarred sliced jalapeño peppers, drained and chopped
8	24	5-inch corn tortillas
2 cups	6 cups	store-bought green enchilada sauce
2 cups (8 ounces)	6 cups (1½ pounds)	low-fat shredded cheese blend (see page 34)
1	3	6-ounce can(s) sliced black olives, drained
3	9	scallions, diced

Spray one (three) 9 × 13-inch baking dish(es) with nonstick cooking spray.

Putting the dinner together

Cook the ground beef in a nonstick pan over medium-high heat until browned. Transfer the meat to a plate lined with paper towels for any excess fat to drain. Set aside. In a large bowl, combine the onion(s), garlic, sour cream, tomatoes, ricotta cheese, and green chiles and stir until incorporated. Set aside.

Spread 1 cup of the enchilada sauce in the bottom of the prepared baking dish(es). Arrange 4 corn tortillas on top of the sauce. Spread half of the ground beef over the tortillas, dividing equally if you are preparing a triple batch. Top with half of the sour cream mixture. Cover the sour cream mixture with 4 more tortillas. Spread the remaining enchilada sauce, shredded cheese, olives, and scallions over the tortillas, dividing equally among the three dishes if you are preparing a triple batch.

For dinner tonight

Preheat the oven to 350°F. Cover the dish with aluminum foil and bake for 45 minutes. Remove the foil and bake for 15 minutes more or until the cheese is melted and bubbly.

To freeze

Cover with plastic wrap and heavy-duty aluminum foil. Label, date, and freeze for up to 3 months. Thaw in the refrigerator before cooking as directed above.

Summertime Barbecue Spareribs

Once in a while on a hot summer day you have to drink an ice-cold soft drink. How about putting some soda in your barbecue? These ribs need to be slow cooked and basted often and are well worth the effort. Serve them with Kahlúa Baked Beans on page 98, Corn Bread Muffins on page 102, and the Layered Strawberry Gelatin Salad on page 100, and you have a complete Dream Dinner.

Serves 6

For One	For Three	Ingredients
6 pounds	18 pounds	pork spareribs
½ teaspoon	1½ teaspoons	kosher salt
½ teaspoon	1½ teaspoons	black pepper
2 teaspoons	6 teaspoons	paprika
2 teaspoons	6 teaspoons	chili powder
1 cup	3 cups	ketchup
¼ cup	¾ cup	Worcestershire sauce
1	3	12-ounce can(s) cola soft drink
¼ cup	¾ cup	apple cider vinegar
1 cup	3 cups	yellow onions, diced

Putting your dinner together

Place the spareribs into a 1-gallon resealable freezer bag. Add the salt, pepper, paprika, and chili powder over the meat and seal tightly. Toss the bag to coat the ribs. Open the bag and add the remaining ingredients.

For dinner tonight

Marinate the meat in the refrigerator for at least 1 hour. Prepare a grill to medium-low heat. Grill the meat on low for 1 to 1½ hours, turning every 10 minutes. Bring the remaining sauce to a boil and hold at a simmer while brushing generously with the sauce while turning.

To freeze

Label, date, and freeze for up to 3 months. Thaw in the refrigerator before cooking as directed above.

Shepherd's Pie

This classic family dinner is a great way to sneak vegetables into a picky eater's diet. If you don't have the time to make your own mashed potatoes, buy the prepared variety available in your grocer's freezer section. This is a wonderful dish to make for new parents—they can warm it up in no time or freeze it for later.

Serves 6

For One	For Three	Ingredients
		nonstick cooking spray
1 pound	3 pounds	lean ground beef, cooked and drained
½ cup	1 cup	yellow onion, diced
1 cup	3 cups	small carrot(s), diced
2 cups	6 cups	celery, diced
1 cup	3 cups	frozen peas
1 cup	3 cups	frozen corn
1 tablespoon	3 tablespoons	all-purpose flour
1 teaspoon	1 tablespoon	dried oregano
1 tablespoon	3 tablespoons	dried parsley
½ teaspoon	1½ teaspoons	kosher salt
½ teaspoon	1½ teaspoons	black pepper
¼ cup	¾ cup	nonfat egg substitute

For One	For Three	Ingredients
¼ cup	¾ cup	red wine
3 cups (1½ pounds)	9 cups (4½ pounds)	prepared mashed potatoes
1 cup (4 ounces)	3 cups (12 ounces)	low-fat shredded cheese blend (see page 34)

Spray one (three) 9 × 13-inch baking dish(es) with nonstick cooking spray.

Putting the dinner together

Spread 2 cups of the meat on the bottom of the prepared baking dish(es). Spread the onion on top, dividing it equally among the three dishes if you are preparing a triple batch. Follow the onion with the carrot(s), celery, peas, and corn in a similar fashion. Set aside. In a bowl, whisk together the flour, oregano, parsley, salt, pepper, eggs, and wine. Spread the flour mixture over the vegetables, dividing it equally among the three dishes if you are preparing a triple batch. Follow with a layer of mashed potatoes and cheese in a similar fashion.

If you are assembling multiples of more than one recipe, pick recipes that use the same meat. For example, make Tried-and-True Lasagne, Shepherd's Pie, and Beef and Corn Enchiladas on the same day, since they all use ground beef.

For dinner tonight

Preheat the oven to 350°F. Bake, uncovered, for 1 to 1½ hours, until the potato crust is golden brown and the vegetables are fork tender.

To freeze

Cover with plastic wrap and heavy-duty aluminum foil. Label, date, and freeze for up to 3 months. Thaw in the refrigerator before cooking as directed above.

New England Pot Roast

Nothing beats a slow-cooked meal, especially when it doesn't require you to be in the kitchen all day. Assemble the ingredients for this pot roast in the crockpot in the morning, and by that evening, your kitchen will be filled with the unmistakable aroma of this beloved dish. **Serves 6**

For One	For Three	Ingredients
		nonstick cooking spray
2 pounds	6 pounds	beef chuck roast, fat removed or trimmed
2 cups	6 cups	baby carrots, raw
1	3	yellow onion(s), quartered
1 cup	3 cups	celery in 3-inch pieces
4	12	red potatoes, halved
2	6	2-inch cabbage wedges
¼ cup	¾ cup	dried onion flakes
2 tablespoons	¼ cup plus 2 tablespoons	apple cider vinegar
1	3	bay leaf (leaves)
2 tablespoons	¼ cup plus 2 tablespoons	olive oil
2 tablespoons	¼ cup plus 2 tablespoons	store-bought horseradish

For One	For Three	Ingredients
3 cups	9 cups	beef broth
½ teaspoon	1½ teaspoons	kosher salt
½ teaspoon	1½ teaspoons	black pepper

Spray one (three) roasting pan(s) with nonstick cooking spray.

Putting the dinner together

Place the chuck roast in the prepared roasting pan(s) or in a crockpot. If you are preparing a triple batch, place the remaining roasts into each of two resealable freezer bags. Add the remaining ingredients to the roasting pan or the crockpot and the resealable freezer bags.

For dinner tonight

Preheat the oven to 325°F. Cover the roasting pan with foil and bake for 2 to 3 hours, or slow-cook in your crockpot on low heat for 6 to 8 hours, until the meat pulls apart easily with a fork.

To freeze

Label, date, and freeze for up to 3 months. Thaw in the refrigerator before cooking as directed above.

Be flexible. If having dinner as a family is a priority, eat at 4:00 P.M. or 8:00 P.M. if you need to. The point is to sit down together and enjoy a healthy dinner at home while building relationships.

Reuben Casserole

This perennial pleaser is a clever take on the classic sandwich. Preparing it casserole style makes fast work of feeding a hungry crowd. **Serves 6**

For One	For Three	Ingredients
		nonstick cooking spray
2 cups	6 cups	nonfat Thousand Island dressing
½ cup	1½ cups	nonfat sour cream
12 slices	36 slices	rye bread, sliced into 1-inch strips
3 cups (1 pound)	9 cups (3 pounds)	sliced pastrami in ½-inch strips
3 cups	9 cups	sauerkraut, drained
2 cups (8 ounces)	6 cups (1½ pounds)	shredded Swiss cheese

Cooking for someone with a food allergy? Make one individual serving of the dinner without the ingredient that causes the allergy for that person. That way everyone can eat the same dinner!

Spray one (three) 9 × 13-inch baking dish(es) with nonstick cooking spray.

Putting the dinner together

In a bowl, combine the dressing and sour cream and mix until well blended. Set aside. Layer one-third of the bread strips on the bottom of the prepared baking dish(es). Layer one-third of the pastrami over the bread, then layer one-third of the sauerkraut over the pastrami, followed by one-third of the sour cream mixture and one-third of the cheese, dividing all of the ingredients equally among the three dishes if you are preparing a triple batch. Repeat the layers again, using one-half of each of the remaining ingredients. Repeat for a third layer, using the remaining bread, meat, sauerkraut, and sauce, and ending with a layer of cheese.

For dinner tonight

Preheat the oven to 350°F. Cover the dish with aluminum foil and bake for 1 hour. Remove the foil and bake for 30 minutes, until the casserole is browned and bubbly and the layers are heated through.

To freeze

Cover the dishes with plastic wrap and heavy-duty aluminum foil. Label, date, and freeze for up to 3 months. Thaw in the refrigerator before cooking as directed above.

Caribbean Blackened Turkey

A turkey tenderloin is transformed on your grill to create a delicious Caribbean themed dinner. Break out the steel-drum music and light a tiki torch.

Serves 6

For One	For Three	Ingredients
2 pounds	8 pounds	turkey breast tenderloin
¼ teaspoon	¾ teaspoon	black pepper
1 teaspoon	3 teaspoons	kosher salt
¼ teaspoon	¾ teaspoon	ground allspice
¼ teaspoon	¾ teaspoon	ground cinnamon
¼ teaspoon	¾ teaspoon	ground cumin
1 tablespoon	3 tablespoons	lite soy sauce
2 tablespoons	6 tablespoons	lime juice
1 teaspoon	3 teaspoons	hot pepper sauce
2 tablespoons	6 tablespoons	apricot preserves
½ cup	1½ cups	minced shallots
2 teaspoons	6 teaspoons	minced garlic
1 teaspoon	3 teaspoons	lime zest

Putting your dinner together

Slice the tenderloin into 1-inch-thick rounds, resulting in 6 slices. Place the turkey slices into a 1-gallon resealable freezer bag. Sprinkle the pepper, salt, allspice, cinnamon, and cumin on the turkey and seal tightly. Toss the bag to coat the slices. Add the remaining ingredients and seal tightly, tossing to coat again.

For dinner tonight

Marinate the turkey in the refrigerator for at least 1 hour. Prepare a grill to medium heat. Remove the turkey from the bag, reserving the marinade, and grill for 5 minutes per side, depending on the thickness. Alternatively, heat an oven broiler to high and spray a broiler pan with cooking spray. Place the turkey on the sprayed pan and broil for 5 minutes per side, depending on the thickness. Meanwhile, boil the remaining marinade for 5 minutes on the stovetop and serve over the turkey tenderloin slices.

To freeze

Label, date, and freeze for up to 3 months. Thaw in the refrigerator before cooking as directed above.

Caribbean Pork over Rice

This dish calls for jerk seasoning, which can be found in the spice section of most grocery stores. You can buy shredded cooked pork in your supermarket's meat department, but it's easy to make it yourself: place a lean pork loin in a crockpot, cover it with canned low-sodium chicken broth, and simmer for eight hours on low. The pork will shred easily when you pull the meat apart with two forks.

Serves 6

For One	For Three	Ingredients
4 cups (1½ pounds)	12 cups (4½ pounds)	shredded cooked pork
2 cups	6 cups	canned chicken broth
½ cup	1½ cups	light unsweetened coconut milk
2 teaspoons	2 tablespoons	jerk seasoning
1 teaspoon	1 tablespoon	grated orange zest
1 cup	3 cups	uncooked white rice for serving
½ cup (4 ounces)	1½ cups (12 ounces)	sliced almonds for garnish

Putting the dinner together

Prepare the rice according to the package directions. In a large bowl, combine the pork, chicken broth, coconut milk, jerk seasoning, and orange zest and stir until incorporated. If you are preparing a triple batch, divide the mixture into three equal portions. Set aside one portion for tonight and divide the other two portions equally between two 1-gallon resealable freezer bags.

For dinner tonight

Heat a skillet over medium-high heat. Add the meat mixture and bring to a boil. The pork should be heated through. Serve over the rice and garnish with the sliced almonds.

To freeze

Place ½ cup of the remaining sliced almonds into each of two 1-quart resealable freezer bags. Place 3 cups cooked and cooled rice in a 1-gallon resealable freezer bag. Place the bags of almonds, rice, and pork into a 1-gallon resealable freezer bag. Repeat with the remaining almonds, rice, and pork. Label, date, and freeze for up to 3 months. Thaw in the refrigerator before cooking as directed above. To reheat the rice, put the rice and ½ cup broth or water in a dish. Cover and cook in the microwave for 1-minute intervals until the broth is absorbed.

Tortillas are a way to use leftovers creatively. Lay out a tortilla, add leftovers, some salsa, and sour cream, and perhaps lettuce or fresh spinach and a slice of cheese. Roll up and serve warm or chilled.

Pork Tenderloin with Pears

Pork, pears, and onions are seasoned to perfection in this dish; just add rice or pasta and you have an elegant dinner party perfectly suited for a small dinner table. Serve this with the Pumpkin Icebox Pie (page 232).

Serves 6

For One	For Three	Ingredients
		nonstick cooking spray
6 (1½ pounds)	18 (4½ pounds)	1-inch-thick slices pork tenderloin
2 cups	6 cups	yellow onions, thinly sliced
1	3	15-ounce can(s) pears with syrup
2 teaspoons	2 tablespoons	minced garlic
¼ cup	¾ cup	dried cranberries
½ cup	1½ cups	white wine
¼ cup	¾ cup	balsamic vinegar
1 tablespoon	3 tablespoons	olive oil
1 teaspoon	1 tablespoon	dried thyme
¼ teaspoon	¾ teaspoon	ground nutmeg
½ teaspoon	1½ teaspoons	grated fresh ginger
1 teaspoon	1 tablespoon	kosher salt
1 teaspoon	1 tablespoon	black pepper

Spray one (three) 9 × 13-inch baking dish(es) with nonstick cooking spray.

Putting the dinner together

Place 6 pork loin slices in the prepared baking dish(es) or in a crockpot. If you are preparing a triple batch, divide the remaining slices equally between two 1-gallon resealable freezer bags. Set aside. In a large bowl, combine the remaining ingredients and mix until incorporated. If you are preparing a triple batch, pour one-third of the mixture into the crockpot or baking dish, and divide the remaining mixture equally between the two bags filled with the pork tenderloin.

For dinner tonight

If you are using a baking dish, preheat the oven to 325°F. Cover the dish with aluminum foil and bake for 2 hours or until the internal temperature of the pork reads 160°F on a meat thermometer. Alternatively, slow-cook the pork in the crockpot on low heat for 5 to 6 hours, until the pork is tender.

To freeze

Label, date, and freeze for up to 3 months. Thaw in the refrigerator before cooking as directed above.

Cider-Braised Pork Loin Chops

This sweet and savory pork dish is great for entertaining, as it gives the impression that you've spent a lot of time in the kitchen. **Serves 6**

For One	For Three	Ingredients
6 (1½ pounds)	18 (4½ pounds)	1-inch-thick slices pork tenderloin
1	3	15-ounce can(s) diced tomatoes with juice
3	9	Granny Smith apples, peeled, cored, and sliced 1 inch thick
1½ pounds	4½ pounds	new potatoes, halved and boiled for 10 minutes
1	3	yellow onion(s), sliced into ¼-inch-thick slices
1 cup	3 cups	chicken broth
¾ cup	2¼ cups	frozen apple juice concentrate
⅓ cup	1 cup	apple cider vinegar
1 tablespoon	3 tablespoons	minced garlic
2 teaspoons	2 tablespoons	olive oil
¼ cup	¾ cup	low-fat yogurt-based spread or butter, melted
⅓ cup	1 cup	light brown sugar, packed
2 teaspoons	2 tablespoons	dried parsley

For One	For Three	Ingredients
½ teaspoon	1½ teaspoons	dried thyme
pinch	3 pinches	allspice

Putting the dinner together

If you are preparing a triple batch, set aside 6 slices of pork loin for one batch, and divide the remaining pork loin equally between two resealable freezer bags.

In a large bowl, combine the remaining ingredients and stir gently until incorporated. If you are preparing a triple batch, set aside one-third of the mixture and divide the remaining mixture equally between the resealable freezer bags holding the pork slices.

Thaw dinners completely in the refrigerator; they will taste better when reheated.

For dinner tonight

Heat a large skillet or a flameproof casserole over high heat. Spoon 2 to 3 teaspoons of the liquid mixture into the pan, then add the pork loin slices. Cook for 2 to 3 minutes per side. Reduce the heat to medium and add the remaining mixture, stirring gently to mix. Cover and cook for 30 to 45 minutes, until the pork is tender. Serve.

To freeze

Label, date, and freeze for up to 3 months. Thaw in the refrigerator before cooking as directed above.

Chicken in Herbed Mustard Sauce

Fennel gives this basic garlic and white wine marinade a distinct flavor. Roasted-garlic mashed potatoes are the perfect accompaniment for this family-style dinner. It is also delicious served over egg noodles or rice.

Serves 6

For One	For Three	Ingredients
⅓ cup	1 cup	lemon juice
⅓ cup	1 cup	white wine
⅓ cup	1 cup	Dijon mustard
1 tablespoon	3 tablespoons	minced garlic
1 tablespoon	3 tablespoons	dried rosemary
2 tablespoons	¼ cup plus 2 tablespoons	whole black peppercorns
1 teaspoon	1 tablespoon	fennel seeds
½ teaspoon	1½ teaspoons	red pepper flakes
1 cup	3 cups	chicken broth
1 tablespoon	3 tablespoons	olive oil
2 tablespoons	¼ cup plus 2 tablespoons	cornstarch
6	18	4-ounce boneless, skinless chicken breast halves

Putting the dinner together

In a large bowl, combine the lemon juice, wine, mustard, garlic, rosemary, peppercorns, fennel seeds, and red pepper flakes and stir. Set aside. In a small bowl, combine the chicken broth, olive oil, and cornstarch and mix until incorporated. Combine the wine mixture and the cornstarch mixture in a resealable freezer bag. If you are preparing a triple batch, divide the liquid mixture equally among the three resealable freezer bags. Add 6 chicken breast halves to each bag and mix gently.

For dinner tonight

Refrigerate the chicken until ready to cook. Heat a skillet over medium-high heat. Add the chicken and marinade. Bring the marinade to a boil and cook the chicken for 5 minutes per side, allowing the sauce to thicken. Serve.

To freeze

Label, date, and freeze for up to 3 months. Thaw in the refrigerator before cooking as directed above.

A meat-based dinner will hold longer thawed in the refrigerator than a starch-based dinner (with rice, pasta, beans, or bread). A good rule of thumb to follow: Allow 2 to 3 days for thawing in your refrigerator, and then be sure to cook and consume the meal within the next 3 to 4 days.

Herb-Tomato Chicken

Chicken breasts topped with fresh tomatoes, a creamy sauce, and seasoned breading, this is a delicious dish to share at your next potluck dinner.

Serves 6

For One	For Three	Ingredients
		nonstick cooking spray
6	18	4-ounce boneless, skinless chicken breast halves
¼ cup	¾ cup	canned cream of celery soup
2 teaspoons	2 tablespoons	minced garlic
1 tablespoon	3 tablespoons	Dijon mustard
6 slices	18 slices	¼-inch-thick tomato slices
½ teaspoon	1½ teaspoons	kosher salt
1 teaspoon	1 tablespoon	black pepper
½ cup	1½ cups	seasoned bread crumbs
2 tablespoons	¼ cup plus 2 tablespoons	dried parsley
2 teaspoons	2 tablespoons	dried rosemary

Spray one (three) 9 × 13-inch baking dish(es) with nonstick cooking spray.

Putting the dinner together

Place the chicken breasts in the prepared baking dish(es). Set aside. In a bowl, combine the soup, garlic, and mustard and stir until well mixed. Spread equal amounts of the sauce on each chicken breast. Top with tomato slices. If you are preparing a triple batch, divide the ingredients equally among the three dishes. Set aside. In a small bowl, combine the salt, pepper, bread crumbs, parsley, and rosemary. Sprinkle equal amounts of the herb mixture evenly over the chicken and tomatoes.

For dinner tonight

Preheat the oven to 375°F. Bake the dish, uncovered, for 40 to 50 minutes, until the internal temperature of the chicken is 165°F.

To freeze

Cover each dish with plastic wrap and heavy-duty aluminum foil. Label, date, and freeze for up to 3 months. Thaw in the refrigerator before cooking as directed above.

Swiss Chicken

This dish of chicken cutlets covered with Swiss cheese and cooked in a mushroom soup and wine mixture will bring back memories of your grandmother's comforting chicken dish. It freezes beautifully. **Serves 6**

For One	For Three	Ingredients
		nonstick cooking spray
6	18	4-ounce boneless, skinless chicken breast halves
6 slices (5 ounces)	18 slices (1 pound)	Swiss cheese
1	3	10-ounce can(s) cream of mushroom soup
1 cup	3 cups	white wine
2 cups	6 cups	seasoned dry stuffing mix
¾ stick (3 ounces)	2 sticks (8 ounces)	low-fat yogurt-based spread or butter, melted

Spray one (three) 9 × 13-inch baking dish(es) with nonstick cooking spray.

Putting your dinner together

Place 6 chicken breasts in the prepared baking dish(es) and cover each cutlet with a slice of cheese. Set aside. In a bowl stir together the soup and wine until combined. Spoon equal amounts of the soup mixture over each chicken cutlet. Sprinkle equal amounts of the stuffing mix and melted spread over each dish.

For dinner tonight

Preheat the oven to 350°F. Bake the dish, uncovered, for 1 hour or until the internal temperature of the chicken reaches 165°F.

To freeze

Cover each dish with plastic wrap and heavy-duty aluminum foil. Label, date, and freeze for up to 3 months. Thaw in the refrigerator before cooking as directed above.

Chicken Cordon Bleu

This chicken dish is the one to make when company comes. If you have it on hand in the freezer, elegant entertaining is as easy as popping this dish in the oven and tossing a salad.

Serves 6

For One	For Three	Ingredients
		nonstick cooking spray
6	18	4-ounce boneless, skinless chicken breast halves
6 (3 ounces)	18 (9 ounces)	ham, thinly sliced
6 (5 ounces)	18 (1 pound)	Swiss cheese, sliced
½ cup	1½ cups	canned cream of chicken soup
¼ cup	¾ cup	white wine
¼ cup	¾ cup	nonfat sour cream
1 tablespoon	3 tablespoons	Dijon mustard
1 cup (4 ounces)	3 cups (12 ounces)	mushrooms, sliced
1 teaspoon	1 tablespoon	minced garlic
¼ teaspoon	¾ teaspoon	ground nutmeg
1 teaspoon	1 tablespoon	kosher salt
½ teaspoon	1½ teaspoons	black pepper
2	6	scallions, chopped

Spray one (three) 9 × 13-inch baking dish(es) with nonstick cooking spray.

Putting the dinner together

Place the chicken breasts on a plastic cutting board. Arrange a slice of ham and Swiss cheese on top of each one. Roll each chicken breast tightly and secure with a toothpick. Place the rolled breasts in the prepared baking dish(es). In a bowl, combine the soup, wine, sour cream, mustard, mushrooms, garlic, nutmeg, salt, and pepper and mix thoroughly. Pour the mixture over the chicken, dividing the mixture equally among the three dishes if you are preparing a triple batch. Sprinkle with the scallions.

If you are gentle and your chicken is completely thawed, you can skewer your rolled chicken with a raw spaghetti noodle and you won't have to warn your dinner partners about the toothpick.

For dinner tonight

Preheat the oven to 375°F. Bake, uncovered, for 45 minutes or until the internal temperature of the chicken reaches 165°F.

To freeze

Cover the dishes with plastic wrap and heavy-duty aluminum foil. Label, date, and freeze for up to 3 months. Thaw in the refrigerator before cooking as directed above.

Chicken Parmesan

This Italian restaurant standard is so easy to put together at home, you want to add the Chianti bottles and red-checkered tablecloths. For a side dish, boil some pasta, toss with a little olive oil and a handful of Parmesan, and top with fresh chopped parsley. Allow at least 2 hours for the chicken to marinate before baking or freezing it. **Serves 6**

For One	For Three	Ingredients
		nonstick cooking spray
½ cup	1½ cups	nonfat Italian dressing
6	18	4-ounce boneless, skinless chicken breast halves
1 cup (4 ounces)	3 cups (12 ounces)	grated Parmesan cheese
⅔ cup	2 cups	seasoned bread crumbs
1 teaspoon	1 tablespoon	paprika
1 teaspoon	1 tablespoon	sugar
1 teaspoon	1 tablespoon	kosher salt
1 teaspoon	1 tablespoon	black pepper
2 cups	6 cups	store-bought marinara sauce

Spray one (three) 9 × 13-inch baking dish(es) with nonstick cooking spray.

Putting the dinner together

Pour the Italian dressing in a bowl and add the chicken. Marinate in the refrigerator for at least 2 hours. Meanwhile, in a shallow bowl, mix together the Parmesan, bread crumbs, paprika, sugar, salt, and pepper. Spread the marinara sauce in the bottom of the prepared baking dish(es). Dredge the marinated chicken in the bread crumb mixture. Place 6 chicken breasts in the prepared baking dish(es) and sprinkle equally with the bread crumb mixture.

For dinner tonight

Preheat the oven to 350°F. Bake, uncovered, for 1 hour or until the internal temperature of the chicken reaches 165°F.

To freeze

Cover with plastic wrap and heavy-duty aluminum foil. Label, date, and freeze for up to 3 months. Thaw in the refrigerator before cooking as directed above.

Timeline for a 6:00 p.m. Dinner

5:00 P.M. Put dinner in the oven. You can put it in earlier at a lower temperature if needed. A good rule of thumb is to add 25 extra baking minutes for every 25°F you lower the temperature.

5:40 P.M. Set the table and empty the dishwasher at same time. Put on music and turn the TV off.

5:45 P.M. Make a side dish such as an easy salad, sliced fruit, rice, or pasta.

Teriyaki Chicken

Once boiled, ginger-soy marinade for this dish makes a delicious sauce for the chicken. Serve it with fluffy rice and mandarin oranges. **Serves 6**

For One	For Three	Ingredients
1 cup	3 cups	lite soy sauce
½ cup	1½ cups	sugar
½ cup	1½ cups	white wine
zest of 1	zest of 3	orange(s), grated
1 teaspoon	1 tablespoon	grated fresh ginger
1 teaspoon	1 tablespoon	minced garlic
¼ teaspoon	¾ teaspoon	red pepper flakes
6	18	4-ounce boneless, skinless chicken breast halves

Putting your dinner together

In a bowl, combine all the ingredients except the chicken and stir until incorporated. Pour the marinade into a resealable freezer bag, dividing it equally among three if you are preparing a triple batch. Add 6 chicken breasts to each bag and seal.

For dinner tonight

Refrigerate the chicken until ready to cook. Prepare a hot grill or broiler or heat and spray a nonstick pan with vegetable oil over high heat. Cook the chicken for 10 minutes per side or until the internal temperature of the chicken reaches 165°F. Meanwhile, boil the marinade in a saucepan for 5 minutes. Serve with the chicken.

To freeze

Label, date, and freeze for up to 3 months. Thaw in the refrigerator before cooking as directed above.

When deciding what type of wine to cook with, unless noted in the recipe, it is up to your personal taste. If you like things on the sweet side use a sweeter wine. If you prefer more of the wine flavor use a dry Chardonnay or Cabernet. You are the chef!

Chicken Stir-Fry

Chopping vegetables takes a bit of time, but preparing a triple batch saves you time in the long run. Steam some rice and slice some cucumbers and place in a bowl with seasoned rice vinegar, and you have a theme dinner party. Don't forget the fortune cookies! **Serves 6**

For One	For Three	Ingredients
¼ cup	¾ cup	sesame oil
½ cup	1½ cups	honey
½ cup	1½ cups	lite soy sauce
3 teaspoons	½ cup plus 1 tablespoon	minced garlic
⅛ teaspoon	⅜ teaspoon	red pepper flakes
6	18	scallions, chopped
1	3	green pepper(s), sliced into ¼-inch pieces
1	3	red pepper(s), sliced into ¼-inch pieces
1	3	large carrot(s), sliced into ¼-inch pieces
6	18	4-ounce boneless, skinless chicken breast halves, sliced into 1-inch-thick pieces

Putting your dinner together

Make each batch separately. In a bowl, combine the sesame oil, honey, soy sauce, garlic, and red pepper flakes and stir to combine. Pour soy sauce mixture into each of three resealable freezer bags. Add 6 chicken breasts to each bag.

For dinner tonight

Allow the chicken to marinate for 4 to 5 hours. Heat a large skillet over high heat. Add the chicken and the marinade and cook for 5 minutes, just until the chicken loses its color. Remove the chicken with a slotted spoon and set aside. Add the scallions, bell peppers, and carrot(s) to the hot pan and cook for 1 minute. Return the chicken to the pan and cook for 4 to 5 more minutes, until heated through, and serve.

To freeze

Place each batch of vegetables in a separate resealable freezer bag. Place the bags containing the chicken and marinade into the vegetable bag and seal tightly. Label, date and freeze for up to 3 months. Thaw in the refrigerator before cooking as directed above.

Spicy Lime Chicken

You can transform a simple chicken breast into a savory, fiery, and succulent dinner with a combination of limes, garlic, and cayenne. Serve this with Black Bean and Rice Salad (page 96) or over white rice. **Serves 6**

For One	For Three	Ingredients
½ cup	1½ cups	low-sodium canned chicken broth
zest of 1	zest of 3	lime(s)
⅓ cup	⅔ cup	lime juice
2 tablespoons	¼ cup plus 2 tablespoons	olive oil
2 tablespoons	6 tablespoons	dried parsley
1 teaspoon	1 tablespoon	minced garlic
1 tablespoon	3 tablespoons	dried onion flakes
1 teaspoon	1 tablespoon	dried thyme
1 teaspoon	1 tablespoon	kosher salt
¼ teaspoon	¾ teaspoon	cayenne pepper
1 teaspoon	1 tablespoon	black pepper
6	18	4-ounce boneless, skinless chicken breast halves

Putting the dinner together

In a 1-gallon resealable freezer bag, combine all the ingredients except the chicken and stir thoroughly. If you are preparing a triple batch, divide the ingredients between two resealable freezer bags. Add 6 chicken breasts to each bag.

Zesting fruit is easy. Use the smallest holes of the grater and remove just the color of the peel. Move the grater over the fruit to remove all the color. The oils in the peel are what you want instead of the white part of the peel, which tends to be bitter. The oils are what impart the intense flavors.

For dinner tonight

Heat a skillet over high heat. Add the chicken and liquid to the pan and cook the chicken for 3 minutes on each side. Reduce the heat to medium and cook until the internal temperature of the chicken is 165°F, 5 to 8 minutes per side.

To freeze

Label, date, and freeze for up to 3 months. Thaw in the refrigerator before cooking as directed above.

Crockpot Jambalaya

Serve this dish over steamed white or brown rice for a no-fuss meal. Stir in some shelled and cooked shrimp just before serving if you like.

Serves 6

For One	For Three	Ingredients
6	18	4-ounce boneless, skinless chicken breast halves, cut into thirds
½ pound	1½ pounds	turkey kielbasa, sliced on the diagonal into 2-inch pieces
1	3	15-ounce can(s) diced tomatoes, with juice
1 cup	3 cups	green or red bell pepper(s), diced into 1-inch pieces
1 cup	3 cups	yellow onion(s), diced into 1-inch pieces
1 cup	3 cups	celery, diced into 1-inch pieces
1 cup	3 cups	whole pitted black olives
½ cup	1½ cups	chicken broth
1 tablespoon	3 tablespoons	cayenne pepper
1 teaspoon	1 tablespoon	dried oregano
1 teaspoon	1 tablespoon	Cajun seasoning
1 teaspoon	1 tablespoon	minced garlic

Putting your dinner together

Combine the ingredients in a crockpot. If you are preparing a triple batch, mix the ingredients together in a large bowl and place one-third of the mixture in a crockpot. Divide the remaining mixture equally between two resealable freezer bags.

For dinner tonight

Set the crockpot on low and cook for 6 to 7 hours, until Serve over rice.

To freeze

Slide each bag into a second resealable freezer bag. Label, date, and freeze for up to 3 months. Thaw in the refrigerator before cooking as directed above.

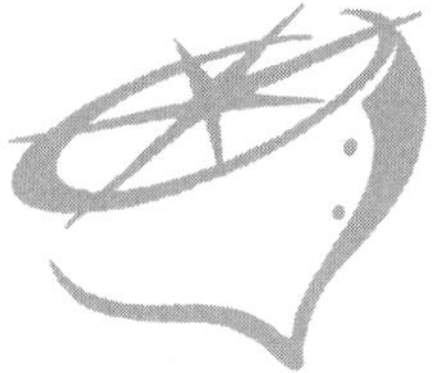

Mango Curry Chicken

Spoon these succulent pieces of chicken over a mound of fluffy rice and sprinkle with chopped cashew nuts and fresh cilantro for a dramatic presentation. The sweet and savory sauce is addictive, so triple the recipe to indulge a desire on a moment's notice. **Serves 6**

For One	For Three	Ingredients
½ cup	1½ cups	yellow onions, chopped
1 tablespoon	3 tablespoons	sugar
1 teaspoon	1 tablespoon	curry powder
1 teaspoon	1 tablespoon	ground coriander
¼ teaspoon	¾ teaspoon	ground cinnamon
⅛ teaspoon	¼ teaspoon	cayenne pepper
½ teaspoon	1½ teaspoons	turmeric
½ teaspoon	1½ teaspoons	kosher salt
pinch	3 pinches	ground cloves
6	18	4-ounce boneless, skinless chicken breast halves, cut into thirds
½	1½	15-ounce can(s) diced tomatoes with juice
½ cup	1½ cups	store-bought mango chutney

Putting the dinner together

In a large bowl, combine the ingredients and stir well to combine. If you are preparing a triple batch, use one-third tonight and divide the remainder between two resealable freezer bags.

For dinner tonight

Spoon the chicken mixture into a crockpot. Cook in the crockpot on the low setting for 4 hours. Alternatively, heat a skillet over medium heat and cook the mixture for 20 minutes or until the chicken is cooked through. Serve over rice and sprinkle with ½ cup chopped cashew nuts and ¼ cup fresh chopped cilantro, if desired.

To freeze

Label, date, and freeze the bags for up to 3 months. Thaw in the refrigerator before cooking and serve as directed above.

Chicken with Red Potatoes

Ranch dressing makes the perfect creamy sauce for tender chicken and potatoes. Red potatoes have such thin skins that there's no need to peel them, and the skin is full of nutrients.

Serves 6

For One	**For Three**	**Ingredients**
		nonstick cooking spray
1½ pounds	**4½ pounds**	**red potatoes, quartered and blanched in boiling water for 3 minutes**
1 cup	**3 cups**	**red bell pepper(s), sliced into ¼-inch pieces**
6	**18**	**4-ounce boneless, skinless chicken breast halves, cut into thirds**
1 cup	**3 cups**	**nonfat sour cream**
1	**3**	**10.5-ounce can(s) cream of chicken soup**
1	**3**	**1-ounce package(s) powdered ranch salad dressing mix**
1 teaspoon	**1 tablespoon**	**garlic salt**

Spray one (three) 9 × 13-inch baking dish(es) with nonstick cooking spray.

Putting the dinner together

Spread the potatoes in the bottom of the prepared baking dish(es). Layer the bell pepper(s) and chicken breasts on top of the potatoes. Set aside. If you are preparing a triple batch, layer an equal amount of potatoes, bell peppers, and chicken in each of the three dishes.

In a large bowl, combine the sour cream, soup, ranch dressing mix, and salt and stir thoroughly. Spread over the chicken, dividing the mixture equally among the three dishes if you are preparing a triple batch.

For dinner tonight

Preheat the oven to 350°F. Cover the dish with aluminum foil and bake for 1½ hours, until browned and bubbly.

To freeze

Cover with plastic wrap and heavy-duty aluminum foil. Label, date, and freeze for up to 3 months. Thaw in the refrigerator before cooking as directed above.

Let's Talk

Light a candle.

- It creates a warm atmosphere.
- It suggests a special time.
- The flame provides soft light and a focal point for our attention.
- It's naturally relaxing and soothing.

Crispy Picnic Chicken

This chicken is delicious hot or cold, making it the ultimate portable dinner. Bake and serve it immediately, or chill and take it on a picnic. Slide it into a picnic basket with the Quick Raspberry Pie (page 238) and head to the nearest grassy meadow or your own backyard. **Serves 6**

For One	For Three	Ingredients
		nonstick cooking spray
8	24	cut-up chicken fryer pieces
1 cup	3 cups	nonfat egg substitute
2 cups	6 cups	crushed Rice Krispies cereal
½ teaspoon	1½ teaspoons	garlic powder
½ teaspoon	1½ teaspoons	kosher salt
½ teaspoon	1½ teaspoons	black pepper

Spray one (three) 9 × 13-inch baking dish(es) with nonstick cooking spray.

Putting the dinner together

Place the chicken pieces in a large bowl. Pour the egg substitute over the chicken and stir to coat thoroughly. Set aside. In another bowl, combine the crushed Rice Krispies, garlic powder, salt, and pepper.

Roll each piece of the chicken in the Rice Krispies mixture, coating thoroughly, and place the chicken in the prepared baking dish(es). If you are preparing a triple batch, arrange 8 pieces of chicken in each dish, placing a mixture of parts in each one. Spray chicken pieces lightly with vegetable spray.

For dinner tonight

Preheat the oven to 350°F. Bake, uncovered, for 1 hour or until the chicken reaches 165°F on a meat thermometer. You can serve it hot or refrigerate overnight and serve it chilled.

To freeze

Cover the dishes with plastic wrap and heavy-duty aluminum foil. Label, date, and freeze for up to 3 months. Thaw in the refrigerator before baking as directed above.

Chicken and Black Bean Chili

This hearty dish is perfect to serve on cool fall weekends after sporting activities or winter weekends après ski. Offer sour cream and shredded Cheddar cheese as garnishes.

Serves 6

For One	For Three	Ingredients
		nonstick cooking spray
3	9	15-ounce can(s) black beans, drained
2 cups	6 cups	cooked chicken, diced
2 teaspoons	2 tablespoons	minced garlic
1 cup	3 cups	yellow onions, diced
¼ cup, or to taste	¾ cup, or to taste	canned jalapeños, drained and sliced
1	3	28-ounce can(s) diced tomatoes with juice
2 tablespoons	¼ cup plus 2 tablespoons	chili powder
1 tablespoon	3 tablespoons	ground cumin
2 teaspoons	2 tablespoons	ground coriander

Spray one (three) 9 × 13-inch baking dish(es) with nonstick cooking spray.

Putting the dinner together

In a large bowl, combine the ingredients and stir. Transfer to the prepared baking dish(es) or a crockpot or stockpot. If you are preparing a triple batch, divide the remainder equally between two resealable freezer bags.

For dinner tonight

Preheat the oven to 325°F. Bake the dish, covered, for 2 hours. Alternatively, turn the crockpot to low and cook for 5 to 6 hours. To cook in a stockpot, simmer the chili over low heat for 2 to 3 hours, stirring often, until thickened.

To freeze

Label, date, and freeze for up to 3 months. Thaw in the refrigerator before cooking as directed above.

Dream Chicken

For moist and tender chicken breast, boil a large pot of water and add boneless, skinless chicken breasts with a teaspoon each of garlic powder and lemon pepper. Return the water to a boil and cook for 5 to 10 minutes, or until the chicken is cooked through. Remove the chicken from the water, cool, and cut up with a knife or kitchen scissors. Cook more than you need for your recipe, and freeze the remainder in resealable freezer bags for later use.

Chicken Potpie

Few dishes measure up to a home-cooked potpie. Not only is it the ultimate comfort food, it's also a great dish to make when there's chicken (or turkey) left over from dinner the night before. We use carrots and potatoes here, but you can just as easily use turnips and parsnips for a slightly different version.

Serves 6

For One	For Three	Ingredients
		nonstick cooking spray
1 cup	3 cups	large carrot(s), diced
1 cup	3 cups	celery, diced
2 cups	6 cups	frozen potatoes, diced
¼ cup	¾ cup	crumbled cooked bacon
1 cup	3 cups	yellow onion(s), diced
2 cups	6 cups	cooked chicken or turkey, diced
1 cup	3 cups	chicken broth
1	3	10-ounce can(s) cream of chicken soup
¼ cup	¾ cup	all-purpose flour
1 teaspoon	1 tablespoon	dried basil
1 teaspoon	1 tablespoon	dried tarragon

For One	For Three	Ingredients
1 teaspoon	1 tablespoon	kosher salt
½ teaspoon	1½ teaspoons	black pepper
1	3	9-inch round(s) store-bought pie dough

Spray one (three) deep dish pie plate(s) with nonstick cooking spray.

Putting the dinner together

In a large bowl, combine the ingredients and mix until incorporated. Spoon equal amounts of the mixture into the prepared baking dish(es). Set aside.

Using a rolling pin, gently roll and stretch the dough, on a lightly floured work surface, that will hang 1 inch over the edges of the pie plate. Lay the dough over the pie plate and crimp the edges.

Make three or four slits on the surface of the crust with a butter knife.

Having dinner together is a tangible way for parents to show they care by investing time in talking with and listening to their children. Children also learn about their parents' values just by listening to them talk about the day's events.

For dinner tonight

Preheat the oven to 350°F. Cover the dish with aluminum foil and bake for 1½ hours. Remove the foil and bake for 10 minutes more or until the crust is golden.

To freeze

Cover each dish with plastic wrap and heavy-duty aluminum foil. Label, date, and freeze for up to 3 months. Thaw in the refrigerator before cooking as directed above.

Chicken and Artichoke Casserole

A little curry powder lends a hint of warmth to this soothing casserole, a Dream Dinners favorite. Use low-sodium cream of chicken soup if you are watching your sodium intake.

Serves 6

For One	For Three	Ingredients
		nonstick cooking spray
1½ cups	4½ cups	uncooked white rice
1 cup	3 cups	marinated artichoke hearts, drained
3	9	scallions, chopped
2 cups	6 cups	cooked chicken in 1-inch pieces
1	3	10-ounce can(s) cream of chicken soup
½ cup	1½ cups	nonfat mayonnaise
1 tablespoon	3 tablespoons	lemon juice
½ teaspoon	1½ teaspoons	black pepper
½ teaspoon	1½ teaspoons	curry powder
2 cups	6 cups	seasoned croutons
1 cup (4 ounces)	3 cups (12 ounces)	low-fat shredded cheese blend (see page 34)
1 tablespoon	3 tablespoons	dried parsley

Spray one (three) 9 × 13-inch baking dish(es) with nonstick cooking spray.

Putting the dinner together

Place the rice on the bottom of the prepared baking dish(es). Layer with the artichokes, scallions, and chicken, dividing the ingredients equally among the three dishes if you are preparing a triple batch. Set aside. In a bowl, combine the soup, mayonnaise, lemon juice, pepper, and curry powder and stir until incorporated. Spread the soup mixture over the chicken mixture. Top with the croutons, cheese, and parsley.

For dinner tonight

Preheat the oven to 375°F. Bake for 1 hour or until the cheese is melted and bubbly.

To freeze

Cover the dishes with plastic wrap and heavy-duty aluminum foil. Label, date, and freeze for up to 3 months. Thaw in the refrigerator before cooking as directed above.

Cooking Rice in Large Quantities

Cook large batches of rice all at the same time, cool in the refrigerator uncovered in a shallow pan, and place in resealable freezer bags to freeze, or use for times-three cooking as needed. A good rule of thumb for cooking rice is to put 2 parts cold water to 1 part rice in a saucepan over high heat on your stovetop. Cover and bring to a boil. Leave covered and remove from the heat. Let it sit, covered, for 20 minutes or until the water is absorbed. The rice will not be quite done—tender, but not completely soft.

Cheesy Chicken and Rice Casserole

If you have a family full of picky eaters to feed, this is the dinner for you. Prepare this meal on a busy weeknight, toss a green salad, and dinner is served.

Serves 6

For One	For Three	Ingredient
		nonstick cooking spray
1½ cups	4½ cups	uncooked white rice
1	3	16-ounce bag(s) frozen corn kernels
2 cups (8 ounces)	6 cups (1½ pounds)	low-fat shredded cheese blend (see page 34)
2 cups	6 cups	cooked chicken breast, diced
1 cup	3 cups	yellow onion(s), diced
1 tablespoon	3 tablespoons	sugar
2 teaspoons	2 tablespoons	kosher salt
2 teaspoons	2 tablespoons	chili powder
2 teaspoons	2 tablespoons	paprika
2 cups	6 cups	nonfat milk

Spray one (three) 9 × 13-inch baking dish(es) with nonstick cooking spray.

Putting the dinner together

Put the rice, corn, cheese, chicken, and onion(s) in a large bowl and mix together. Combine the sugar, salt, and chili powder. Divide the rice mixture equally among the three dishes if you are preparing a triple batch. Sprinkle equal amounts of the chili powder mixture over each. Sprinkle the paprika on top.

For dinner tonight

Preheat the oven to 350°F. Pour the milk into the baking dish. Bake, covered with aluminum foil, for 1½ hours or until the cheese begins to bubble.

To freeze

Pour 2 cups milk into each of two resealable freezer bags and seal. Place one bag of milk on top of each baking dish. Cover the dishes with plastic wrap and heavy-duty aluminum foil. Label, date, and freeze for up to 3 months.

Thaw in the refrigerator. Pour the milk into the baking dish and bake as directed above.

We always use yellow onions. One medium yellow onion will yield 1 cup diced onion. To easily prepare an onion, cut it down the middle, through the root. Slice off the root, peel each side, and then slice or dice as needed.

Baked Chicken Salad

Layers of vegetables and chicken are baked in a tangy soy sauce, then topped with crunchy chow mein noodles in this baked "salad." Serve fresh sliced cucumbers and good bread with this salad for a hearty lunch or dinner.

Serves 6

For One	For Three	Ingredients
		nonstick cooking spray
3 cups	9 cups	cooked chicken meat, diced
3 tablespoons	½ cup plus 1 tablespoon	lemon juice
1 teaspoon	1 tablespoon	kosher salt
¼ cup	¾ cup	soy sauce
1 tablespoon	3 tablespoons	sesame oil
1 cup	3 cups	fat-free sesame dressing
2 cups	6 cups	celery, chopped
1 cup	3 cups	green bell pepper(s), chopped
6	18	scallions, chopped
1 cup	3 cups	carrots, diced
½ cup (2 ounces)	1½ cups (6 ounces)	almonds, sliced
2 cups	6 cups	chow mein noodles

Spray one (three) 9 × 13-inch baking dish(es) with nonstick cooking spray.

Putting the dinner together

In a large bowl, combine the chicken, lemon juice, salt, soy sauce, sesame oil, and sesame dressing and mix gently. Add the celery, bell pepper(s), scallions, and carrots and mix. Spoon the mixture into the prepared baking dish. If you are preparing a triple batch, use one-third tonight and divide the remainder between two resealable freezer bags.

For dinner tonight

Preheat the oven to 350°F. Sprinkle the top of the baking dish with the almonds and Chinese noodles. Bake, uncovered, for 30 to 45 minutes, until the top is bubbly and crisp.

To freeze

Combine 2 cups of chow mein noodles and ½ cup of almonds in each of two resealable freezer bags. Place one in each of the bags filled with chicken and vegetables. Label, date, and freeze for up to 3 months. Thaw in the refrigerator before cooking as directed above.

Foods That Freeze Best

- **Uncooked proteins,** like chicken, pork, and beef.
- **Fresh carrots, zucchini, onions, and celery,** but *not* fresh potatoes.
- **Mayonnaise does not freeze.** Substitute cream cheese or sour cream if a recipe calls for mayonnaise as a sauce base.
- When converting a regular recipe to a freezer recipe, **use extra liquid, stock, or milk.**

Arroz con Pollo

Arroz con pollo, or rice with chicken, is a classic Spanish one-pot meal.

Serves 6

For One	For Three	Ingredients
		nonstick cooking spray
1 cup	3 cups	uncooked white rice
1	3	15-ounce can(s) black beans, drained
1 cup	3 cups	frozen corn kernels
6	18	4-ounce boneless, skinless chicken breast halves
1 teaspoon	1 tablespoon	kosher garlic salt
¼ teaspoon	¾ teaspoon	black pepper
½ cup	1½ cups	chicken broth
1 cup	3 cups	store-bought salsa
1 cup	3 cups	store-bought marinara sauce
½ cup	1½ cups	red bell pepper(s), sliced
½ cup	1½ cups	scallions, chopped
¼ cup	¾ cup	fresh cilantro, chopped
¼ teaspoon	¾ teaspoon	ground cumin

For One	For Three	Ingredients
1 teaspoon	1 tablespoon	minced garlic
1 cup (4 ounces)	3 cups (12 ounces)	low-fat shredded cheese blend (see page 34)

Spray one (three) 9 × 13-inch baking dish(es) with nonstick cooking spray.

Putting the dinner together

Prepare the rice according to the package directions. Spread the rice over the bottom of the prepared baking dish(es). Layer the beans, corn, and chicken over the rice and sprinkle with the salt and pepper. Set aside. In a large bowl, combine the chicken broth, salsa, marinara sauce, bell pepper(s), scallions, cilantro, cumin, and garlic and mix thoroughly. Pour the mixture in equal amounts over the chicken in each of the three baking dishes if you are preparing a triple batch. Sprinkle cheese over each baking dish.

For dinner tonight

Preheat the oven to 350°F. Bake for 45 minutes to 1 hour, until the internal temperature of the chicken breasts reaches 165°F.

To freeze

Cover the dishes with heavy-duty aluminum foil. Label, date, and freeze for up to 3 months. Thaw in the refrigerator before cooking as directed above.

Stuffed French Bread

A perfect dish for potluck or picnic, this foil-baked filled bread couldn't be easier to make. If you can't find chicken sausage, pork is fine; just cook it, remove the casing, and crumble.

Serves 6

For One	For Three	Ingredients
1	3	loaf (loaves) French bread, split in half lengthwise
1 stick (4 ounces)	3 sticks (12 ounces)	low-fat yogurt-based spread or butter
½ cup (4 ounces)	1½ cups (12 ounces)	nonfat cream cheese
½ cup	1½ cups	yellow onion(s), diced
1 tablespoon	3 tablespoons	dried parsley
1 tablespoon	3 tablespoons	poppy seeds
1 cup	3 cups	precooked chicken sausage, cut into ½-inch pieces
20 slices	60 slices	cooked Canadian bacon
9 slices (5 ounces)	27 slices (1 pound)	Swiss cheese

Putting the dinner together

Place a 1 (3) foot-long piece(s) of aluminum foil on a clean workspace and place the bottom half (halves) of the loaf (loaves) on it. Set aside. In a large bowl, cream together the spread, cream cheese, onion(s), parsley, and poppy seeds with a handheld electric mixer. Blend the sausage into the cream cheese mixture. Spread the mixture evenly on the bread halves. Layer the Canadian bacon on the bottom half of the loaf and top with the Swiss cheese slices, dividing the bacon and cheese equally among the three loaves if you are preparing a triple batch. Place the top half of the bread over the toppings and wrap tightly in foil.

For dinner tonight

Preheat the oven to 400°F or heat a grill to medium heat. Bake the bread in the aluminum foil for 15 minutes. Unwrap and slice into 2-inch slices.

To freeze

Label, date, and freeze for up to 3 months. Thaw at room temperature before cooking as directed above.

Parmesan-Crusted Fish Fillets

You can use a variety of white flaky fish for this recipe. Take care not to overcook the fish, as it can get tough and chewy when the natural oils are baked out. Tilapia is one of our favorite fishes for this dish, since it freezes particularly well and children like it. **Serves 6**

For One	For Three	Ingredients
		nonstick cooking spray
6 tablespoons	1 cup plus 2 tablespoons	all-purpose flour
6 tablespoons	1 cup plus 2 tablespoons	yellow cornmeal
1 teaspoon	1 tablespoon	garlic powder
1 tablespoon	3 tablespoons	dried parsley
1 tablespoon	3 tablespoons	dried basil
1 teaspoon	1 tablespoon	kosher salt
½ teaspoon	1½ teaspoons	black pepper
½ cup	1½ cups	nonfat egg substitute
½ cup	1½ cups	low-fat buttermilk
6	18	4-ounce tilapia fillets
2 tablespoons	¼ cup plus 2 tablespoons	olive oil
½ cup (2 ounces)	1½ cups (6 ounces)	grated Parmesan cheese

Spray one (three) 9 × 13-inch baking dish(es) with nonstick cooking spray.

Putting your dinner together

In a large shallow bowl, combine the flour, cornmeal, garlic powder, parsley, basil, salt, and pepper and mix thoroughly. Set aside. In a separate shallow bowl, mix together the egg substitute and buttermilk. Dip the fish fillets into the egg mixture and then dredge in the flour mixture until completely covered. Place the breaded fillets in the prepared baking dish(es), arranging 6 in each if you are preparing a triple batch. Sprinkle with the olive oil and Parmesan.

For dinner tonight

Preheat the oven to 450°F. Bake, uncovered, for 8 to 10 minutes, until the fish is crisp and golden brown.

To freeze

Cover the dishes with plastic wrap and heavy-duty aluminum foil. Label, date, and freeze for up to 3 months. Thaw at room temperature before cooking as directed above.

Sake and Soy Marinated Salmon

Salmon is incredibly flavorful and versatile. It is also quite healthful, as it contains important omega-3 fatty acids, which are an essential part of our diet.

Serves 6

For One	For Three	Ingredients
		nonstick cooking spray
½ cup	1½ cups	soy sauce
½ cup	1½ cups	sake, sherry, or white wine
2 tablespoons	¼ cup plus 2 tablespoons	minced fresh ginger
2 tablespoons	¼ cup plus 2 tablespoons	lemon juice
3 tablespoons	½ cup plus 1 tablespoon	sugar
2 tablespoons	¼ cup plus 2 tablespoons	pickled ginger
3	9	scallions, chopped
1 tablespoon	3 tablespoons	sesame seeds
¼ cup	¾ cup	dried shiitake mushrooms
2 pounds	6 pounds	boneless, skinless salmon fillets

Spray one (three) 9 × 13-inch baking dish(es) with nonstick cooking spray.

Putting your dinner together

Combine the ingredients in a resealable freezer bag. Marinate the fish for up to 8 hours. If you are preparing a triple batch, combine equal amounts of each ingredient in each of three resealable freezer bags.

For dinner tonight

Preheat the oven to 450°F. Remove the salmon from the marinade with a slotted spoon. Wrap it in heavy-duty aluminum foil and roast for 8 to 10 minutes. Alternatively, prepare a hot grill and cook the fillets for about 5 minutes, until the meat flakes away when poked with a fork. Meanwhile, bring the marinade to a full boil in a saucepan, reduce the heat, and simmer until reduced by half, about 10 minutes. Drizzle the sauce over the salmon and serve.

To freeze

Label, date, and freeze for up to 3 months. Thaw in the refrigerator before cooking as directed above.

Roasted Mediterranean Halibut

Halibut is a firm white fish. A good rule of thumb is to roast it for 7 to 8 minutes per inch of thickness of the steak, making sure the oven has been preheated before roasting. Buy pitted Kalamata olives and use kitchen scissors to cut the basil and sun-dried tomatoes to make fast work of this delicious dish.

Serves 6

For One	For Three	Ingredients
		nonstick cooking spray
6	18	4-ounce boneless, skinless halibut fillets
1½ teaspoons	1 tablespoon plus 1½ teaspoons	minced garlic
¼ cup	¾ cup	fresh basil, chopped
¼ cup	¾ cup	olive oil
¼ cup	¾ cup	pitted Kalamata olives, chopped
1 tablespoon	3 tablespoons	capers, drained
1½ teaspoons	1 tablespoon plus 1½ teaspoons	caper juice
1 tablespoon	3 tablespoons	oil-packed sun-dried tomatoes, drained and chopped
zest and juice of 1	zest and juice of 3	lemon(s)

Spray one (three) 9 × 13-inch baking dish(es) with nonstick cooking spray.

Putting the dinner together

Place the halibut steaks in the prepared baking dish(es). Set aside. In a large bowl, combine the remaining ingredients except the lemon zest and stir until incorporated. Pour the mixture evenly over the halibut, dividing it equally among the dishes if tripling the batch. Sprinkle with the zest.

For dinner tonight

Preheat the oven to 450°F. Roast the halibut in a baking dish, uncovered, for 7 to 8 minutes, until a fork flakes the center with ease.

To freeze

Cover the dishes with plastic wrap and heavy-duty aluminum foil. Label, date, and freeze for up to 3 months. Thaw at room temperature before cooking as directed above.

Dill Shrimp with Angel Hair Pasta

These dill-flavored shrimp make an excellent appetizer on their own, but arrange them atop a bed of just-cooked pasta and dinner is served! If you freeze a package of dry pasta with the shrimp, all of the components for dinner will be at your fingertips.

Serves 6

For One	For Three	Ingredients
1 pound	3 pounds	large shrimp, deveined and peeled
¼ cup	¾ cup	white wine
¼ cup	¾ cup	olive oil
2 tablespoons	¼ cup plus 2 tablespoons	fresh parsley, chopped
2 tablespoons	¼ cup plus 2 tablespoons	scallions, chopped
2 tablespoons	¼ cup plus 2 tablespoons	fresh dill, chopped
1 tablespoon	3 tablespoons	Dijon mustard
½ teaspoon	1½ teaspoons	black pepper
1 teaspoon	1 tablespoon	minced garlic
1	3	bay leaf (leaves)
1 teaspoon	3 teaspoons	kosher salt
2 pounds	6 pounds	dried angel hair pasta

Putting the dinner together

Combine all the ingredients except the pasta in a resealable freezer bag. Divide the ingredients equally among three resealable freezer bags if you are preparing a triple batch. Seal the bag(s) tightly and squeeze gently to mix the ingredients together.

For dinner tonight

Place one bag in the refrigerator to marinate until ready to cook. Meanwhile, cook the pasta in a large pot of boiling water according to the package directions. Heat a skillet over high heat. Add the shrimp mixture and marinade and cook until the shrimp turn pink, about 5 minutes. Place the pasta on a large rimmed platter, spoon the shrimp onto the pasta, and serve.

To freeze

Place the pasta in a separate resealable freezer bag and seal tightly. Place the bag of pasta and a bag of shrimp and marinade into a third resealable freezer bag. Label, date, and freeze for up to 3 months. Thaw at room temperature before cooking as directed above.

Shrimp Creole

Planning a Mardi Gras party? This is the perfect dish for a festive gathering. Serve this with Cajun Dirty Rice on page 88.

Serves 6

For One	For Three	Ingredients
1 cup (4 ounces)	3 cups (12 ounces)	button or cremini mushrooms, sliced
¼ cup	¾ cup	olive oil
1 cup	3 cups	celery, diced
¼ cup	¾ cup	all-purpose flour
½ cup	1½ cups	store-bought barbecue sauce
½	1½	15-ounce can(s) diced tomatoes with juice
¼ teaspoon	¾ teaspoon	cayenne pepper
1 teaspoon	1 tablespoon	kosher salt
½ cup	1½ cups	yellow onion(s), diced
1 pound	3 pounds	large shrimp, deveined and peeled

Putting the dinner together

Combine the ingredients in a resealable freezer bag, dividing them equally among three bags if you are preparing a triple batch. Seal tightly and squeeze gently to mix.

For dinner tonight

Place one bag in the refrigerator to marinate until ready to cook dinner. Heat a large skillet over medium-high heat until hot. Add the shrimp and marinade. Cook until the shrimp turns pink, about 5 minutes. Serve immediately over rice.

To freeze

Label, date, and freeze for up to 3 months. Thaw at room temperature before cooking as directed above.

Let's Talk

Turn off the television and play some fun music, which creates ambience and triggers memories.

Let each family member take turns picking the dinner music.

- Music triggers memories.
- Music creates ambience.
- Music softly fills the room, preventing long silences that can be awkward.

Greatest Grub Ever Crab Chili

This recipe originated with The Greatest Grub Ever company and uses their Greatest Grub Ever Buffalo Hot Sauce. This sauce will knock your socks off. It can be purchased online at www.thegreatestgrubever.com, or you can substitute another favorite hot sauce. Serve with a dollop of sour cream.

Serves 6

For One	For Three	Ingredients
1 cup	3 cups	yellow onion(s), diced
1 cup	3 cups	red bell pepper(s), diced
1 cup	3 cups	yellow bell pepper(s), diced
1 cup	3 cups	orange bell pepper(s), diced
½ cup	1½ cups	jarred jalapeños, drained and diced
1 teaspoon	1 tablespoon	red pepper flakes
½ cup	1½ cups	Greatest Grub Ever Buffalo Hot Sauce or any favorite brand
1 teaspoon	1 tablespoon	dried oregano
1 teaspoon	1 tablespoon	kosher salt
½ teaspoon	1½ teaspoons	ground cumin
1 tablespoon	3 tablespoons	chili powder
1	3	15-ounce can(s) black beans, drained
2 pounds	6 pounds	crabmeat

Putting the dinner together

In a large bowl, combine the onion(s), bell peppers, jalapeños, red pepper flakes, and hot sauce. If you are preparing a triple batch, divide the mixture between a large bowl and two resealable freezer bags. Combine the oregano, salt, cumin, chili powder, and beans in another bowl. Place one-third in each of two additional resealable freezer bags. Divide the crabmeat equally between the mixing bowl and a third set of resealable freezer bags.

For dinner tonight

Heat a skillet over high heat. Add the vegetable mixture and cook for 10 minutes over medium-high heat, stirring often. Add the bean mixture and cook for 5 minutes more. Add the crab and simmer for 10 minutes. Serve hot with sour cream.

To freeze

Place one each of the pepper mixture, bean mixture, and crab into 1-gallon resealable freezer bags. Label, date, and freeze for up to 3 months. Thaw at room temperature before cooking as directed above.

Vegetable Chili

This number-one favorite winter dinner will get you through the cold weather months. Serve the chili with Corn Bread Muffins (page 102). Bulgur wheat can be found in the bulk food or natural foods section of the grocery store.

Serves 6

For One	For Three	Ingredients
½ cup	1½ cups	bulgur wheat
¼ cup	¾ cup	olive oil
1 cup	3 cups	yellow onion(s), chopped
2 cups	6 cups	celery, diced
1 cup	3 cups	large carrot(s), diced
1 tablespoon	3 tablespoons	minced garlic
¼ cup	¾ cup	tomato paste
1½ cups	4½ cups	white wine
½ cup	1½ cups	red bell pepper(s), diced
½ cup	1½ cups	green bell pepper(s), diced
1 cup	3 cups	zucchini, diced
1	3	15-ounce can(s) diced tomatoes with juice
1	3	15-ounce can(s) kidney beans, drained

For One	For Three	Ingredients
1	3	15-ounce can(s) black beans, drained
4 teaspoons	¼ cup	chili powder
1 tablespoon	3 tablespoons	ground cumin
½ teaspoon	1½ teaspoons	cayenne pepper
2 teaspoons	2 tablespoons	dried basil
1 teaspoon	1 tablespoon	dried oregano

Putting the dinner together

In a large bowl, combine the ingredients with 4 (12) cups water. Stir until incorporated. If you are preparing a triple batch, place one-third of the mixture in a crockpot or a large stockpot. Divide the remaining mixture equally between two 1-gallon resealable freezer bags.

For dinner tonight

Cook the chili in the crockpot, on low heat, for 6 to 8 hours, until thickened. Alternatively, cover and simmer over low heat on the stovetop in a stockpot for 2 to 3 hours, until the vegetables are tender.

Dice vegetables no smaller than 1 inch. Frozen dishes with larger chunks of vegetables taste better when reheated.

To freeze

Label, date, and freeze for up to 3 months. Thaw at room temperature before cooking as directed above.

Vegetarian Tamale Pie

This south-of-the-border shepherd's pie is the perfect blend of beans, vegetables, and seasonings, topped with a corn bread crust. Serve it with a big green salad for a quick weeknight meal.

Serves 6

For One	For Three	Ingredients
		nonstick cooking spray
1 cup	3 cups	yellow onion(s), diced
½	1½	green bell pepper(s), chopped
2	6	2.25-ounce can(s) sliced black olives, drained
1	3	15-ounce can(s) black beans, drained
3	9	15-ounce can(s) kidney beans, drained
1 cup	3 cups	frozen corn
3 cups	9 cups	store-bought marinara sauce
2 tablespoons	¼ cup plus 2 tablespoons	sugar
1 tablespoon	3 tablespoons	chili powder
⅛ teaspoon	¼ plus ⅛ teaspoons	cayenne pepper
1	3	15-ounce package(s) corn bread mix
1 cup (4 ounces)	3 cups (12 ounces)	low-fat shredded cheese blend (see page 34)

Spray one (three) 9 × 13-inch baking dish(es) with nonstick cooking spray.

Putting the dinner together

In a large bowl, combine the onion(s), bell pepper(s), half of the olives, the black beans, kidney beans, corn, marinara sauce, sugar, chili powder, and cayenne and mix well to incorporate. Pour into the baking dish, dividing equally among the three dishes if you are preparing a triple batch. Set aside. In a separate bowl, combine 1½ (4½) cups water with the corn bread mix. Spread this mixture evenly over the ingredients in the baking dish(es), dividing it equally among the three dishes if you are preparing a triple batch. Top the corn bread mixture(s) with shredded cheese and the remaining olives.

For dinner tonight

Preheat the oven to 350°F. Bake, uncovered, for 1½ hours or until a toothpick inserted in the corn bread topping comes out clean and the top is golden brown.

To freeze

Cover with plastic wrap and heavy-duty aluminum foil. Label, date, and freeze for up to 3 months. Thaw at room temperature before cooking as directed above.

DESSERTS

Nothing brings family and friends together around the dinner table faster than a homemade dessert. Never mind that you prepared that Pecan Pie (page 236) weeks ago. As it warms in the oven tonight, the aroma is irresistible and its appearance on the table will seem a miracle. That's the beauty of Dream Desserts. When you make three Cinnamon Apple Cakes (page 228), you will have two on hand for those impromptu get-togethers or unexpected invitations to dinner. The minute guests arrive, slide the cake into the oven; they'll think you've been baking all day. Making dessert for a special dinner party doesn't have to take hours, nor does dessert have to be a fancy confection. If you have a big batch of Fresh Peach Sorbet (page 242) in the freezer, serve a scoop with some purchased cookies for a bright end to a wonderful meal. Most of the recipes in this chapter will remind you of classic comfort desserts, some with a twist. There's Rhubarb Cobbler (page 230), a Pumpkin Icebox Pie (page 232) that you can serve straight from the freezer, and Dreamy Peanut Butter and Chocolate Cream Pie (page 234) with a bit of peanut butter added for good measure. Fill your cookie jar—and your freezer—with Grammy's Chocolate Chip Cookies (page 244) for an endless supply of after-school snacks. Whatever the occasion or season, you'll find a sweet treat in this chapter that you'll want to enjoy tonight and have on hand whenever the craving strikes.

Cinnamon Apple Cake

Big chunks of apple and a cinnamon crumb topping make this dense cake a breakfast treat, or the special ending to a dinner. To reduce the amount of oil without sacrificing any moistness, replace half of the oil with applesauce. This cake can be prepared and frozen before baking, then thawed and baked the day you want to serve it. **Serves 6**

For One	For Three	Ingredients
		nonstick cooking spray
1 cup	3 cups	all-purpose flour
1 cup	3 cups	dark brown sugar, packed
1 cup	3 cups	granulated sugar
4 teaspoons	¼ cup	ground cinnamon
¾ cup	2¼ cups	canola oil
1 teaspoon	1 tablespoon	kosher salt
½ teaspoon	1½ teaspoons	ground ginger
1 teaspoon	3 teaspoons	baking soda
1 teaspoon	3 teaspoons	baking powder
2	6	Granny Smith apples, peeled and sliced into bite-sized pieces
1 cup	3 cups	buttermilk
¼ cup	¾ cup	nonfat egg substitute

Spray one (three) 9 × 13-inch baking dish(es) with nonstick cooking spray.

Putting the dessert together

In a large bowl, combine the flour, brown sugar, granulated sugar, half of the cinnamon, the oil, salt, and ginger. Transfer 1½ cups of this mixture to a small bowl and add the remaining cinnamon to it. Stir until incorporated. Set aside for the topping. Add the baking soda, baking powder, apples, buttermilk, and egg substitute to the flour mixture, stirring until just combined. Do not over-mix. Pour into the prepared baking dish(es), dividing the mixture equally among the three dishes if you are preparing a triple batch. Sprinkle the reserved topping over the apple mixture.

For dessert tonight

Preheat the oven to 350°F. Bake for 1½ hours or until the cake is set and the topping is golden brown. Serve warm or at room temperature.

To freeze

Cover with plastic wrap and heavy-duty aluminum foil. Label, date, and freeze for up to 3 months. Thaw at room temperature before baking as directed above.

Rhubarb Cobbler

This cobbler has become an expected part of our Easter Sunday dinner. With two more in the freezer, we can still enjoy rhubarb's unmistakable tart and tangy flavor when its season has passed. **Serves 6**

For One	For Three	Ingredients
		nonstick cooking spray
1	3	1-pound 2.25-ounce box(es) yellow cake mix
5 cups (1¾ pounds)	15 cups (5 pounds)	fresh or frozen rhubarb, coarsely chopped
1 cup	3 cups	sugar
½ teaspoon	1½ teaspoons	ground cinnamon
1	3	3-ounce box powdered raspberry gelatin
zest of 1	zest of 3	lemon(s), grated
½ cup	1½ cups	low-fat yogurt-based spread or butter, melted

Spray one (three) 9 × 13-inch baking dish(es) with nonstick cooking spray.

Putting the dessert together

Spread the dry cake mix in the bottom of the prepared baking dish(es). Spread the rhubarb over the top of the cake mix. Sprinkle the sugar, cinnamon, and gelatin over the rhubarb. Scatter the lemon zest on top and drizzle evenly with the melted spread.

For dessert tonight

Preheat the oven to 350°F. Bake, uncovered, for 1 hour or until the top is golden brown and crisp.

To freeze

Cover with plastic wrap and heavy-duty aluminum foil. Label, date, and freeze for up to 3 months. Thaw at room temperature before baking as directed above.

Pumpkin Icebox Pie

The perfect fall dessert, enjoyed right from your freezer. Nonfat nondairy whipped topping and nonfat vanilla ice cream can be used with no loss in taste but far fewer calories. Be sure to use canned pumpkin, not pumpkin pie mix.

Serves 6

For One	For Three	Ingredients
		nonstick cooking spray
2 cups	6 cups	crushed graham crackers
¼ cup	¾ cup	low-fat yogurt-based spread or butter, melted
1¼ cups plus 2 tablespoons	4 cups plus 2 tablespoons	sugar
1	3	15-ounce can(s) 100% pure pumpkin
1 teaspoon	1 tablespoon	kosher salt
1 teaspoon	1 tablespoon	ground ginger
½ teaspoon	1½ teaspoons	ground nutmeg
1½ teaspoons	4½ tablespoons	ground cinnamon
2 cups	6 cups	nonfat nondairy whipped topping
½ teaspoon	1½ teaspoons	vanilla extract
3 cups	9 cups	nonfat vanilla ice cream, softened
½ cup (2 ounces)	1½ cups (6 ounces)	chopped pecans

Spray one (three) 9 × 13-inch baking dish(es) with nonstick cooking spray.

Putting the pie together

In a large bowl, combine the graham cracker crumbs, melted spread, and sugar and stir thoroughly until well mixed. Press evenly into the bottom of the prepared baking dish(es), dividing the mixture equally among the three dishes if you are preparing a triple batch. Set aside. Combine the pumpkin, salt, ginger, nutmeg, and cinnamon in a large bowl, gently folding the ingredients together until well mixed. Spread evenly over the crust, dividing the filling equally among the three dishes if you are preparing a triple batch. In a large bowl, combine the whipped topping, vanilla, and ice cream and stir until incorporated. Spread evenly over the pumpkin layer, dividing equally among the three if you are preparing a triple batch, and sprinkle with the pecans.

For dessert tonight

Cover with plastic wrap and freeze until ready to serve. Remove the pie from the freezer 15 minutes before serving and cut into squares.

To freeze

Cover with plastic wrap and foil. Label, date, and freeze for up to 3 months. Serve as directed above.

Dreamy Peanut Butter and Chocolate Cream Pie

Go ahead and make three batches at a time of this dreamy dessert: one for tonight, one for a friend, and one to serve from the freezer to your unexpected company.

Serves 8

For One	For Three	Ingredients
1 cup	3 cups	chocolate syrup
1	3	store-bought graham cracker crust(s)
1½ cups (12 ounces)	4½ cups (2¼ pounds)	nonfat cream cheese
1½ cups	4½ cups	sugar
1½ cups	4½ cups	low-fat nondairy whipped topping
1½ cups	4½ cups	peanut butter
¼ cup (1 ounce)	¾ cup (3 ounces)	peanuts, chopped

Putting the dessert together

Spread ½ cup of the chocolate syrup into the bottom of the crust(s). Set aside. In a large bowl, blend the cream cheese and sugar together with a handheld electric mixer on medium speed, until fluffy. Add the whipped topping and peanut butter and mix well. Pour the mixture into the crust, dividing it equally among the three crusts if you are preparing a triple batch. Mound the mixture slightly in the middle. Drizzle another ½ cup of chocolate syrup over the pie(s) and sprinkle each with nuts. Freeze overnight.

For dinner tonight

Serve frozen.

To freeze

Cover with foil, forming a dome to prevent smashing the pie, and place in a deep rigid container with a lid. Label, date, and freeze for up to 3 months. Serve as directed above.

In a Manner of Speaking

Make practicing manners fun by using family "codes" to signal a missed manner. For example:

Elbows off the table: "The Eiffel tower is leaning."

Napkin in your lap: "Are your legs cold?"

Closed mouth when chewing: "How's your seafood?"

Need to wipe your face: "Are you feeling a little crummy?"

Use your fork, not your spoon: "Poke it or slop it?"

Pecan Pie

For the holidays, we like to serve this in its intended pie shape. But it can also be cut into bars and packed in the kids' lunch boxes. **Serves 6 to 8**

For One	For Three	Ingredients
		nonstick cooking spray
1	3	frozen 9-inch piecrust(s)
2 cups (8 ounces)	6 cups (1½ pounds)	pecan pieces
½ cup	1½ cups	corn syrup
1 cup	3 cups	dark brown sugar, packed
½ cup	1½ cups	nonfat egg substitute
¼ cup	¾ cup	low-fat yogurt-based spread or butter, melted
1 teaspoon	1 tablespoon	vanilla extract
½ teaspoon	1½ teaspoons	kosher salt
¼ cup	¾ cup	cocoa powder

Spray one (three) 9 inch pie plate(s) with nonstick cooking spray.

Putting the dessert together

Place a round of piecrust in the pie plate(s) and spread just to the edges. Spread the pecans evenly over the crust, dividing them equally among the three crusts if you are preparing a triple batch. Set aside. In a large bowl, whisk together the corn syrup, brown sugar, egg substitute, spread, vanilla, salt, and cocoa powder. Pour the mixture over the pecans, dividing it equally among the three pie plates if you are preparing a triple batch.

For dessert tonight

Preheat the oven to 350°F. Bake for 30 minutes. Cool completely before cutting into bars.

To freeze

Cover with plastic wrap and foil. Label, date, and freeze for up to 3 months. Thaw at room temperature before baking as directed above.

Quick Raspberry Pie

This can be made with any berries, so long as they are fresh. Though it can't be frozen, this pie is still a dream because it takes just minutes to prepare and is ready to eat in 1 hour. Stephanie's great-grandma Bessie made the topping while the kids picked the berries. **Serves 6**

For One	For Three	Ingredients
3 cups	**9 cups**	**fresh raspberries, plus extra for garnish**
1	**3**	**store-bought graham cracker crust(s)**
1	**3**	**14-ounce can(s) nonfat sweetened condensed milk**
3 tablespoons	**9 tablespoons**	**lemon juice**

Putting the dessert together

Arrange the berries on the bottom of the pie crust(s). Set aside. In a small bowl, whisk together the condensed milk and the lemon juice until the milk thickens, 2 to 3 minutes. Pour over the berries and chill, garnished with a few berries, in the refrigerator for at least 1 hour. Serve.

Cooking and Baking for the Holidays

Here are some tips that help make holiday cooking and baking less stressful. When preparing food the Dream Dinners way, you'll always have something delicious on hand for last-minute visitors.

Create the same menu for each entertaining season.

Big crowd entertaining can be easy if you choose two or three recipes as your signature dinners for that season, triple-batch assemble them, and freeze.

As a rule, all cookies and cakes can be made ahead in big batches and frozen, baked or unbaked, for use the day of (or the day before) the big event.

Muffin batters can be made, poured into paper-lined muffin tins, and frozen. When the batter is completely frozen, remove the paper liners filled with frozen batter from the tins and place in freezer bags. No need to thaw; just pop them back into the muffin tins, reduce the original cooking temperature by 25°F, and bake, adding approximately 30 extra minutes to the original cooking time. Muffins are done when a toothpick inserted in the center comes out clean.

Frozen Mandarin Orange Parfait

Whether you make one or three of these delicious pies, you use only one mixing bowl to combine the ingredients for each layer. This dish is versatile—it makes a wonderful side dish for a barbecue or an unexpected dessert.

Serves 6

For One	For Three	Ingredients
		nonstick cooking spray
2 cups	6 cups	crushed Ritz crackers
¼ cup	¾ cup	low-fat yogurt-based spread or butter, melted
¼ cup	¾ cup	sugar
1 cup	3 cups	low-fat nondairy whipped topping
2	6	15-ounce can(s) mandarin oranges, drained
⅔ cup	2 cups	frozen orange juice concentrate, thawed
3 tablespoons	½ cup plus 1 tablespoon	lemon juice
1	3	14-ounce can(s) nonfat sweetened condensed milk

Spray one (three) 9 × 13-inch baking dish(es) with nonstick cooking spray.

Putting the dessert together

In a bowl, combine the Ritz crackers, spread, and sugar. Press the mixture into the baking dish(es) to form the crust, dividing the mixture equally among the three dishes if you are preparing a triple batch. Set aside. Combine the whipped topping and the mandarin oranges in the same bowl. Spread the mixture evenly over the crust, dividing it equally among the three dishes if you are preparing a triple batch. Combine the orange juice, lemon juice, and condensed milk in the same bowl. Pour the mixture over the whipped topping, dividing it equally if you are preparing a triple batch. Spread evenly with a rubber spatula.

For dessert tonight

Cover with plastic wrap and freeze. Serve frozen, cut into squares.

To freeze

Cover with plastic wrap and foil. Label, date, and freeze for up to 3 months. Serve as directed above.

Fresh Peach Sorbet

You can buy simple syrup at your local grocery store or make it yourself by combining 1 cup water and 2 cups sugar in a small saucepan. Bring to a boil while stirring. Reduce the heat and continue to stir until the sugar dissolves. Cool to room temperature. **Serves 6**

For One	For Three	Ingredients
1 pound	3 pounds	peaches, peeled and cut into 1-inch pieces
1 cup	3 cups	simple syrup
juice of 1	juice of 3	lime(s)
1 tablespoon	3 tablespoons	fresh mint, finely chopped

Putting the sorbet together

Combine the peaches, syrup, lime juice, and mint in the bowl of an electric mixer fitted with the whisk attachment. Mix on medium speed until the ingredients are thoroughly incorporated.

Pour the mixture into a 6- to 8-cup plastic container(s), dividing it equally among three if you are preparing a triple batch. Seal tightly.

For dessert tonight

The sorbet can be placed in the freezer in the plastic container. Serve frozen. Alternatively, pour the contents into an ice cream maker and follow the manufacturer's instructions.

To freeze

Label, date, and freeze for up to 3 months.

Grammy's Chocolate Chip Cookies

Stephanie's grammy was known and loved for her light-as-air cookies. The secret is the cream of tartar.

Makes 2 dozen

For One	For Three	Ingredients
1 cup	3 cups	low-fat yogurt-based spread or butter
1 cup	3 cups	butter-flavored vegetable shortening
1 cup	3 cups	dark brown sugar, packed
1 cup	3 cups	granulated sugar
½ cup	1½ cups	nonfat egg substitute
2 teaspoons	2 tablespoons	vanilla extract
4 cups	12 cups	all-purpose flour
1 tablespoon	3 tablespoons	cream of tartar
2 teaspoons	2 tablespoons	baking soda
1 teaspoon	1 tablespoon	kosher salt
2 cups	6 cups	chocolate chips
1 cup (4 ounces)	3 cups (12 ounces)	walnut pieces, optional

Putting the dessert together

In the bowl of an electric mixer, blend the spread, shortening, brown sugar, and granulated sugar on medium speed until light and fluffy. Add the egg substitute and vanilla and blend until mixed well. Gradually add the flour, cream of tartar, baking soda, and salt while the mixer is running. Remove the bowl from the mixer, add the chocolate chips and walnuts, if using, and mix with a wooden spoon just until combined.

For dessert tonight

Spray two jelly roll pans with vegetable spray. Preheat the oven to 350°F. Spread the dough into the jelly roll pans and bake for 20 to 30 minutes, until the dough is set. Remove from the oven and cut into bars. Cool and remove the bars from the pan. Alternatively, preheat the oven to 375°F. Scoop 1-inch balls from the mix using a small ice cream scoop and arrange on the prepared baking sheets, 2 inches apart. Bake for 10 minutes. Remove the cookies from the sheet while still warm and cool them on a rack or waxed paper.

To freeze

Place the dough in two resealable freezer bags. Label, date, and freeze for up to 3 months. Thaw at room temperature before baking as directed above.

Harvest Bread

This bread is delicious spread with apple yogurt-based spread or any other fruit yogurt-based spread. The batter can be mixed and baked on the day you want to serve it or baked, frozen, and rewarmed. **Makes 1 loaf**

For One	For Three	Ingredients
		nonstick cooking spray
¼ cup	¾ cup	low-fat yogurt-based spread or butter
1 cup	3 cups	sugar
½ cup	1½ cups	nonfat egg substitute
⅓	1	15-ounce can 100% pure pumpkin
1	3	banana(s), mashed
½ cup	1½ cups	low-fat buttermilk
1 cup	3 cups	all-purpose flour
¾ cup	2¼ cups	whole wheat flour
1 teaspoon	1 tablespoon	baking soda
1 teaspoon	1 tablespoon	ground cinnamon
½ teaspoon	1½ teaspoons	kosher salt
½ teaspoon	1½ teaspoons	ground nutmeg
¼ teaspoon	¾ teaspoon	ground ginger

For One	For Three	Ingredients
¼ teaspoon	¾ teaspoon	ground cloves
¾ cup	2¼ cups	chocolate chips
½ cup (6 ounces)	1½ cups (18 ounces)	walnuts, chopped

Spray one (three) 5 × 10-inch loaf pan(s) with nonstick cooking spray.

Putting the bread together

In a bowl, cream the spread and sugar together with a handheld electric mixer until light and fluffy. Beat in the egg substitute, pumpkin, banana(s), and buttermilk. Add the flour, whole wheat flour, baking soda, cinnamon, salt, nutmeg, ginger, and cloves and mix until combined. Stir in the chocolate chips and walnuts. Pour the batter into the prepared loaf pan(s), dividing the mixture equally among the three pans if you are preparing a triple batch.

For dessert tonight

Preheat the oven to 350°F. Bake for 1 hour and 5 minutes to 1 hour and 10 minutes, until golden brown and the bread springs back when pressed.

To freeze

If freezing before baking, divide the batter equally between two resealable freezer bags. If baking first, cool completely and cover with plastic wrap and foil. Label, date, and freeze for up to 3 months. Thaw before baking and/or serving as directed above.

The Best Banana Bread

My mother always buys the overripe bananas in the sale bin at the supermarket to make this bread. In fact, she met my father by asking for the overripe bananas at her local market! The more ripe the bananas, the more moist the bread. If you find yourself with a surplus of overripe bananas, freeze them in the peel for the next time you want to make this fragrant loaf. This bread can be baked, then frozen, thawed, and baked.

Makes 1 loaf

For One	For Three	Ingredients
		nonstick cooking spray
½ cup	1½ cups	vegetable shortening
1 cup	3 cups	sugar
½ cup	1½ cups	nonfat egg substitute
3	9	bananas, mashed
2 cups	6 cups	all-purpose flour
1 teaspoon	3 teaspoons	baking soda
1 teaspoon	3 teaspoons	kosher salt
½ cup (6 ounces)	1½ cups (18 ounces)	walnuts, chopped

Spray one (three) 5 × 10-inch loaf pan(s) with nonstick cooking spray.

Putting the bread(s) together

In a large bowl, cream together the vegetable shortening and sugar with a handheld electric mixer. Beat in the egg substitute and bananas. Gradually add the flour, baking soda, and salt and mix until combined. Stir in the walnuts. Pour the batter into the prepared loaf pan(s), dividing equally among the three pans if you are preparing a triple batch.

For bread today

Preheat the oven to 350°F. Bake for 1 hour and 5 minutes to 1 hour and 10 minutes, until golden brown and the bread springs back when pressed.

To freeze

If freezing before baking, divide the remaining batter equally between two resealable freezer bags. Label, date, and freeze for up to 3 months. Thaw at room temperature before baking as directed above. If baking first, cool completely and cover with plastic wrap and foil. Label, date, and freeze for up to 3 months.

Grandma Rue's Peanut Butter Fingers

Grandma Rue, Tina's mom, who was called Grandma Rue when the grandkids couldn't pronounce her last name, Ruebush, brought these scrumptious cookies to festive occasions, making every gathering extra special. Use just enough milk to make the topping loose enough to drizzle.

Serves 6

For One	For Three	Ingredients
		nonstick cooking spray
½ cup	1½ cups	butter
½ cup	1½ cups	granulated sugar
½ cup	1½ cups	light brown sugar, packed
1 teaspoon	1½ tablespoons	vanilla extract
¼ cup	1½ cups	nonfat egg substitute
⅓ cup	1 cup	peanut butter
½ teaspoon	1½ teaspoons	baking soda
¼ teaspoon	¾ teaspoon	kosher salt
1 cup	3 cups	all-purpose flour
1 cup	3 cups	quick cooking oatmeal

Topping

For One	For Three	Ingredients
1 cup	3 cups	chocolate chips
½ cup	1½ cups	powdered sugar
¼ cup	¾ cup	peanut butter
2 to 4 tablespoons	6 to 12 tablespoons	milk

Spray one (three) 9 × 13-inch baking dish(es) with nonstick cooking spray.

Putting the dessert together

Preheat the oven to 350°F. In a bowl, cream the butter, sugars, and vanilla together with a handheld mixer until smooth. Add the egg substitute and peanut butter and mix until smooth. Mix the dry ingredients in a separate bowl, then combine with the sugar/peanut butter mixture until well blended. (You may need to mix by hand.) Spread the mixture in the bottom of the prepared pan(s). Bake for 20 minutes or until golden brown.

Topping

Sprinkle the chocolate chips over the baked cookie dough mixture immediately after removing the pan(s) from the oven. Let stand for 5 minutes, until the chips have melted. Quickly spread the melted chocolate evenly over the baked cookie dough. Mix powdered sugar, peanut butter, and milk until creamy, adjusting the milk to a desired consistency. Drizzle the topping over the smoothed chocolate.

For dessert tonight

Cut into bars and serve.

To freeze

Cover the pans with plastic wrap and heavy-duty aluminum foil. Label, date, and freeze for up to 1 month. Thaw, cut into bars, and serve.

Freezing: The Basics

Does Freezing Destroy Bacteria and Parasites?

Freezing at 0°F does not destroy microbes—bacteria, yeasts, and molds—present in food; instead it inactivates them. Once thawed these microbes can again become active, multiplying under the right conditions to levels that can lead to foodborne illness. Since they will grow at about the same rate as microorganisms on fresh food, you must handle thawed items as you would any perishable food.

Thorough cooking will destroy all bacteria and parasites.

Freezer Burn

Freezer burn does not make food unsafe, merely dry in spots. It appears as grayish-brown leathery spots and is caused by air reaching the surface of the food. Cut freezer-burned portions away either before or after cooking the food. Heavily freezer-burned foods may have to be discarded for quality reasons.

Color Changes

Color changes can occur in frozen foods. The bright red color of meat as purchased usually turns dark or pale brown depending on the variety. This may be due to lack of oxygen, freezer burn, or long storage.

Freezing doesn't usually cause color changes in poultry. However, the bones and the flesh near them can become dark. Bone darkening results when pigment seeps through the porous bones of young poultry into the surrounding tissues when the poultry is frozen and thawed.

The dulling of color in frozen vegetables and cooked foods is usually the result of excessive drying due to improper packaging or over lengthy storage.

Freeze Rapidly

Freeze food as fast as possible after purchasing or preparing to maintain its quality. Slow freezing creates large, disruptive ice crystals. During thawing, they damage the cells and dissolve emulsions. This causes meat to "drip," or lose its juiciness. Rapid freezing prevents these undesirable large crystals from forming throughout the product because the molecules don't have time to take their positions in the characteristic six-sided snowflake.

Ideally, a food 2 inches thick should freeze completely in about 2 hours. If your home freezer has a "quick-freeze" shelf, use it.

Refrigerator Freezers

If a refrigerator freezing compartment can't maintain zero degrees or if the door is opened frequently, use it for short-term food storage. Eat those foods as soon as possible for best quality. Use a free-standing freezer set at 0°F or below for long-term storage of frozen foods. Keep a thermometer in your freezing compartment or freezer to check the temperature. This is important if you experience a power outage or mechanical problems.

Length of Time

Because freezing keeps food safe almost indefinitely, recommended storage times are for quality only. Refer to the freezer storage chart at the end of this section, which lists optimum freezing times for best quality.

If a food is not listed on the chart, you may determine its quality after defrosting. First check the odor. Some foods will develop a rancid or off odor when frozen too long and should be discarded. Some may not look picture perfect or be of high enough quality to serve alone but may be edible; use them to make soups or stews. Cook raw food and if you like the taste and texture, use it.

Power Outage in Freezer

If there is a power outage and the freezer fails, or if the freezer door has been left ajar by mistake, the food inside may still be safe to use. As long as a freezer with its door ajar is continuing to cool, the foods should stay safe overnight. If a repairman is on the way or it appears the power will be on soon, just don't open the freezer door.

A freezer full of food will usually keep for about two days if the door is kept shut; a half-full freezer will last for about a day. The freezing compartment in a refrigerator may not keep foods frozen as long. If the freezer is not full, quickly group packages together so they will retain the cold more effectively. Separate meat and poultry items from other foods so if they begin to thaw, their juices won't drip onto other foods.

When the power is off, you may want to put dry ice, block ice, or bags of ice in the freezer or transfer foods to a friend's freezer until power is restored. Use an appliance thermometer to monitor the temperature.

When it is freezing outside and there is snow on the ground, the outdoors seems like a good place to keep food until the power comes on; however, frozen food can thaw if it is exposed to the sun's rays even when the temperature is very cold. Refrigerated food may become too warm and food-borne bacteria could grow. The outside temperature could vary hour by hour and the temperature outside will not protect refrigerated and frozen food. Additionally, perishable items could be exposed to unsanitary conditions or to animals. Animals may harbor bacteria or disease; never consume food that has come in contact with an animal.

To determine the safety of foods when the power goes on, check their condition and temperature. If food is partly frozen, still has ice crystals, or is as cold as if it were in a refrigerator (40°F), it is safe to refreeze or use. It's not necessary to cook raw foods before refreezing. *Discard foods that have been warmer than 40°F for more than 2 hours. Discard any foods that have been contaminated by raw meat juices.*

Freezer Storage Chart (0°F)

These guidelines are for quality only. Frozen foods remain safe indefinitely.

Item	Months
Bacon and sausage	1 to 2
Casseroles	2 to 3
Egg whites or nonfat egg substitutes	12
Gravy, meat, or poultry	2 to 3
Ham, hot dogs, and lunch meats	1 to 2
Meat, uncooked roasts	4 to 12
Meat, uncooked steaks or chops	4 to 12
Meat, uncooked ground	3 to 4
Meat, cooked	2 to 3
Poultry, uncooked whole	12
Poultry, uncooked parts	9
Poultry, uncooked giblets	3 to 4
Poultry, cooked	4
Soups and stews	2 to 3
Wild game, uncooked	8 to 12

A Primer on Freezer Styles

There are three types of freezers on the market: upright, chest, and refrigerator-freezer combinations. The upright and refrigerator freezer are available as manual-defrost or frost-free models. *Though less convenient, manual-defrost freezers are more cost efficient. They also maintain higher-quality food than do frostless models because they don't have a fan running to remove the moisture that would turn to frost.* The constant removal of moisture from the freezer could cause freezer burn in improperly wrapped food. Frost-free chest freezers are not available, but frost builds up in chest freezers less readily.

Upright Freezers: These appliances have the same general shape and appearance as home refrigerators. They have one or two outside doors and from three to seven shelves for storing food. Freezers of this type are popular due to their convenience, the small floor space they require, and the ease with which food may be put in or removed. However, more cold air escapes each time the door is opened.

Chest Freezers: Freezers of this type require more floor area than the uprights but are more economical to buy and operate. These freezers lose less cold air each time they're opened. Make sure this type of freezer is equipped with sliding or lift-out baskets to permit easy loading and removal of food.

Refrigerator-Freezer Combination: This is a single appliance with one or two doors. It has one compartment for frozen foods and another for refrigerated foods. The freezing compartments may be above, below, or to one side of the refrigerated area. If selecting this type, be certain that the freezer is a true freezer (will maintain 0°F or less) and not just a freezing compartment.

Labels Times Three

To use these labels, cut them out and photocopy or tape them onto adhesive labels. Affix the labels to plastic bags or baking pans before freezing.

Appetizers

Tri-layered Torte

Thaw completely. Cover with plastic wrap and chill until ready to serve. Remove springform pan, using a spatula to remove the bottom. Slide torte onto a serving plate. Garnish with 1/3 cup parsley or nuts and serve with crackers.

Tri-layered Torte

Thaw completely. Cover with plastic wrap and chill until ready to serve. Remove springform pan, using a spatula to remove the bottom. Slide torte onto a serving plate. Garnish with 1/3 cup parsley or nuts and serve with crackers.

Tri-layered Torte

Thaw completely. Cover with plastic wrap and chill until ready to serve. Remove springform pan, using a spatula to remove the bottom. Slide torte onto a serving plate. Garnish with 1/3 cup parsley or nuts and serve with crackers.

Pesto and Red Pepper Torte

Thaw in the refrigerator overnight. Remove foil and cheesecloth. Garnish with parsley or pine nuts and serve with crackers or cut-up vegetables.

Pesto and Red Pepper Torte

Thaw in the refrigerator overnight. Remove foil and cheesecloth. Garnish with parsley or pine nuts and serve with crackers or cut-up vegetables.

Pesto and Red Pepper Torte

Thaw in the refrigerator overnight. Remove foil and cheesecloth. Garnish with parsley or pine nuts and serve with crackers or cut-up vegetables.

Baked Clam Dip in a Sourdough Bread Bowl

Thaw completely. Preheat oven to 350°F. Keep foil wrapping on, place filled loaf pan on a baking sheet, and bake for 1½ hours or just until filling bubbles around the rim.

Baked Clam Dip in a Sourdough Bread Bowl

Thaw completely. Preheat oven to 350°F. Keep foil wrapping on, place filled loaf pan on a baking sheet, and bake for 1½ hours or just until filling bubbles around the rim.

Baked Clam Dip in a Sourdough Bread Bowl

Thaw completely. Preheat oven to 350°F. Keep foil wrapping on, place filled loaf pan on a baking sheet, and bake for 1½ hours or just until filling bubbles around the rim.

Warm Crab and Artichoke Dip

Thaw completely. Preheat oven to 375°F. Bake, uncovered, for 25 to 30 minutes, until brown and bubbly. Serve with pita triangles, crackers, or fresh vegetables.

Warm Crab and Artichoke Dip

Thaw completely. Preheat oven to 375°F. Bake, uncovered, for 25 to 30 minutes, until brown and bubbly. Serve with pita triangles, crackers, or fresh vegetables.

Warm Crab and Artichoke Dip

Thaw completely. Preheat oven to 375°F. Bake, uncovered, for 25 to 30 minutes, until brown and bubbly. Serve with pita triangles, crackers, or fresh vegetables.

Italian Salsa

Spoon into a serving bowl and serve with tortilla chips or fresh vegetables.

Italian Salsa

Spoon into a serving bowl and serve with tortilla chips or fresh vegetables.

Italian Salsa

Spoon into a serving bowl and serve with tortilla chips or fresh vegetables.

Mu Shu Chicken Wraps

Thaw completely. Preheat oven to 350°F. Cover with foil and bake for 30 minutes. To pan fry, spray a non-stick pan with cooking spray and heat over medium-high heat. Add wraps and cook for 8 to 10 minutes on each side. Add 2 tablespoons of water and cover with a lid. Cook for 2 to 3 minutes more.

Mu Shu Chicken Wraps

Thaw completely. Preheat oven to 350°F. Cover with foil and bake for 30 minutes. To pan fry, spray a non-stick pan with cooking spray and heat over medium-high heat. Add wraps and cook for 8 to 10 minutes on each side. Add 2 tablespoons of water and cover with a lid. Cook for 2 to 3 minutes more.

Mu Shu Chicken Wraps

Thaw completely. Preheat oven to 350°F. Cover with foil and bake for 30 minutes. To pan fry, spray a non-stick pan with cooking spray and heat over medium-high heat. Add wraps and cook for 8 to 10 minutes on each side. Add 2 tablespoons of water and cover with a lid. Cook for 2 to 3 minutes more.

Stuffed Braided Bread

Thaw completely in refrigerator and warm in a 250°F oven for 20 to 30 minutes.

Stuffed Braided Bread

Thaw completely in refrigerator and warm in a 250°F oven for 20 to 30 minutes.

Stuffed Braided Bread

Thaw completely in refrigerator and warm in a 250°F oven for 20 to 30 minutes.

Margarita Slush

Thaw for 1 hour at room temperature or until texture is slush-like. Pour into a pitcher and garnish with fresh lime slices.

Margarita Slush

Thaw for 1 hour at room temperature or until texture is slush-like. Pour into a pitcher and garnish with fresh lime slices.

Margarita Slush

Thaw for 1 hour at room temperature or until texture is slush-like. Pour into a pitcher and garnish with fresh lime slices.

Raspberry Margarita Slush

Thaw for 1 hour at room temperature or until texture is slush-like. Pour into a ½-gallon serving vessel and garnish with fresh lime slices.

Raspberry Margarita Slush

Thaw for 1 hour at room temperature or until texture is slush-like. Pour into a ½-gallon serving vessel and garnish with fresh lime slices.

Raspberry Margarita Slush

Thaw for 1 hour at room temperature or until texture is slush-like. Pour into a ½-gallon serving vessel and garnish with fresh lime slices.

Breakfast and Brunch

Classic Breakfast Strata

Thaw completely. Preheat oven to 350°F. Remove plastic wrap and bake for 1½ hours or until center is set and cheese has melted and is bubbly.

Classic Breakfast Strata

Thaw completely. Preheat oven to 350°F. Remove plastic wrap and bake for 1½ hours or until center is set and cheese has melted and is bubbly.

Classic Breakfast Strata

Thaw completely. Preheat oven to 350°F. Remove plastic wrap and bake for 1½ hours or until center is set and cheese has melted and is bubbly.

English Muffin and Ham Strata

Thaw completely. Pour egg mixture contents over strata and let it soak, overnight, in refrigerator before baking. Preheat oven to 350°F. Remove plastic wrap and bake for 1½ hours or until center is set and cheese is browned and bubbly.

Breakfast Eggs with Potato Crust

Thaw completely. Pour egg mixture over cheese mixture and bake as directed in recipe. Preheat oven to 350°F. Bake until puffed and golden brown, 30 to 45 minutes.

Huevos Rancheros

Thaw completely. Pour egg mixture over the cheese mixture. Preheat oven to 375°F. Cover dish with foil and bake for about 1½ hours or until center is set and cheese is melted and bubbly. Let sit for 10 minutes before serving.

Breakfast Burritos

Thaw completely. Preheat oven to 350°F. Cover dish with foil and bake for 20 minutes. Remove foil and bake for 15 minutes more or until cheese is melted and bubbly.

Breakfast Eggs and Chile Bake

Thaw completely. Preheat the oven to 350°F. Bake 30 to 45 minutes until browned and eggs are set.

Karlene's Cottage Cheese Pancakes

Thaw completely Prepare a griddle with oil. Heat griddle on medium heat, about 375°F. Pour ½ cup of mixture onto griddle for each pancake. Cook pancakes for 1½ minutes per side, or until golden brown, turning once.

Baked Stuffed French Toast

Thaw completely. Preheat oven to 325°F. Bake, uncovered, for 1 hour or until the egg mixture is no longer liquid and toast is browned.

English Muffin and Ham Strata

Thaw completely. Pour egg mixture contents over strata and let it soak, overnight, in refrigerator before baking. Preheat oven to 350°F. Remove plastic wrap and bake for 1½ hours or until center is set and cheese is browned and bubbly.

Breakfast Eggs with Potato Crust

Thaw completely. Pour egg mixture over cheese mixture and bake as directed in recipe. Preheat oven to 350°F. Bake until puffed and golden brown, 30 to 45 minutes.

Huevos Rancheros

Thaw completely. Pour egg mixture over the cheese mixture. Preheat oven to 375°F. Cover dish with foil and bake for about 1½ hours or until center is set and cheese is melted and bubbly. Let sit for 10 minutes before serving.

Breakfast Burritos

Thaw completely. Preheat oven to 350°F. Cover dish with foil and bake for 20 minutes. Remove foil and bake for 15 minutes more or until cheese is melted and bubbly.

Breakfast Eggs and Chile Bake

Thaw completely. Preheat the oven to 350°F. Bake 30 to 45 minutes until browned and eggs are set.

Karlene's Cottage Cheese Pancakes

Thaw completely Prepare a griddle with oil. Heat griddle on medium heat, about 375°F. Pour ½ cup of mixture onto griddle for each pancake. Cook pancakes for 1½ minutes per side, or until golden brown, turning once.

Baked Stuffed French Toast

Thaw completely. Preheat oven to 325°F. Bake, uncovered, for 1 hour or until the egg mixture is no longer liquid and toast is browned.

English Muffin and Ham Strata

Thaw completely. Pour egg mixture contents over strata and let it soak, overnight, in refrigerator before baking. Preheat oven to 350°F. Remove plastic wrap and bake for 1½ hours or until center is set and cheese is browned and bubbly.

Breakfast Eggs with Potato Crust

Thaw completely. Pour egg mixture over cheese mixture and bake as directed in recipe. Preheat oven to 350°F. Bake until puffed and golden brown, 30 to 45 minutes.

Huevos Rancheros

Thaw completely. Pour egg mixture over the cheese mixture. Preheat oven to 375°F. Cover dish with foil and bake for about 1½ hours or until center is set and cheese is melted and bubbly. Let sit for 10 minutes before serving.

Breakfast Burritos

Thaw completely. Preheat oven to 350°F. Cover dish with foil and bake for 20 minutes. Remove foil and bake for 15 minutes more or until cheese is melted and bubbly.

Breakfast Eggs and Chile Bake

Thaw completely. Preheat the oven to 350°F. Bake 30 to 45 minutes until browned and eggs are set.

Karlene's Cottage Cheese Pancakes

Thaw completely Prepare a griddle with oil. Heat griddle on medium heat, about 375°F. Pour ½ cup of mixture onto griddle for each pancake. Cook pancakes for 1½ minutes per side, or until golden brown, turning once.

Baked Stuffed French Toast

Thaw completely. Preheat oven to 325°F. Bake, uncovered, for 1 hour or until the egg mixture is no longer liquid and toast is browned.

Breakfast Apple Bread Pudding

Thaw completely. Pour egg mixture evenly over bread mixture in pan. Preheat the oven to 375°F. Bake for 1½ hours or until set, and top is puffy and browned. Let sit 10 minutes before serving.

Breakfast Apple Bread Pudding

Thaw completely. Pour egg mixture evenly over bread mixture in pan. Preheat the oven to 375°F. Bake for 1½ hours or until set, and top is puffy and browned. Let sit 10 minutes before serving.

Breakfast Apple Bread Pudding

Thaw completely. Pour egg mixture evenly over bread mixture in pan. Preheat the oven to 375°F. Bake for 1½ hours or until set, and top is puffy and browned. Let sit 10 minutes before serving.

Zucchini-Cranberry Bread or Muffins

Thaw completely. Preheat oven to 350°F. Fill prepared Bundt pan with batter, dividing it evenly among three if you are preparing a triple batch. Alternatively, fill prepared muffin tins in a similar fashion. Bake for 1 hour or until bread springs back when pressed lightly.

Zucchini-Cranberry Bread or Muffins

Thaw completely. Preheat oven to 350°F. Fill prepared Bundt pan with batter, dividing it evenly among three if you are preparing a triple batch. Alternatively, fill prepared muffin tins in a similar fashion. Bake for 1 hour or until bread springs back when pressed lightly.

Zucchini-Cranberry Bread or Muffins

Thaw completely. Preheat oven to 350°F. Fill prepared Bundt pan with batter, dividing it evenly among three if you are preparing a triple batch. Alternatively, fill prepared muffin tins in a similar fashion. Bake for 1 hour or until bread springs back when pressed lightly.

Ham and Tomato Biscuits

To reheat, preheat oven to 350°F. Wrap muffins in foil and bake until heated through, 10 to 20 minutes.

Ham and Tomato Biscuits

To reheat, preheat oven to 350°F. Wrap muffins in foil and bake until heated through, 10 to 20 minutes.

Ham and Tomato Biscuits

To reheat, preheat oven to 350°F. Wrap muffins in foil and bake until heated through, 10 to 20 minutes.

Coffee Mocha Punch

Partially thaw mixture and place it into a punch bowl. Add the club soda and ice just before serving and garnish with nutmeg or cinnamon.

Coffee Mocha Punch

Partially thaw mixture and place it into a punch bowl. Add the club soda and ice just before serving and garnish with nutmeg or cinnamon.

Coffee Mocha Punch

Partially thaw mixture and place it into a punch bowl. Add the club soda and ice just before serving and garnish with nutmeg or cinnamon.

Berry Freezer Jam

Serve straight from the freezer. Refreeze any remaining jam.

Berry Freezer Jam

Serve straight from the freezer. Refreeze any remaining jam.

Berry Freezer Jam

Serve straight from the freezer. Refreeze any remaining jam.

Salads, Soups, and Side Dishes

Smoked Turkey and Red Grape Salad

Thaw completely. Arrange romaine lettuce on bottom of serving dish, spoon salad on top and serve.

Smoked Turkey and Red Grape Salad

Thaw completely. Arrange romaine lettuce on bottom of serving dish, spoon salad on top and serve.

Smoked Turkey and Red Grape Salad

Thaw completely. Arrange romaine lettuce on bottom of serving dish, spoon salad on top and serve.

Orzo Salad

Thaw completely. Fluff with a fork and transfer to a serving dish and serve.

Orzo Salad

Thaw completely. Fluff with a fork and transfer to a serving dish and serve.

Orzo Salad

Thaw completely. Fluff with a fork and transfer to a serving dish and serve.

Cremini Mushroom and Caramelized Onion Soup

Thaw completely. Heat a large sauté pan on low and simmer soup on stove for 1 hour, stirring often.

Kielbasa Bean Soup

Thaw completely. Slow-cook in crockpot, set on low heat, for 5 to 6 hours. Alternatively, simmer over low heat on stovetop for 2 hours.

Dreamy French Onion Soup

Thaw completely. Ladle soup into six bowls. Float a slice of toasted sourdough bread on top of soup. Place a slice of Gruyère on each bread slice, then sprinkle with 4 teaspoons grated Parmesan and 4 teaspoons grated fontina. Slide bowls under broiler and broil until the cheese is melted, bubbling, and begins to brown. Garnish with chives and thyme.

Seafood Cioppino

Thaw completely. Cook vegetables and broth in crockpot, set on low, for 5 to 6 hours. Add seafood, stir gently, and cook on low heat for 30 minutes more.

Beef and Cabbage Stew

Thaw completely. Ladle into each of six soup bowls and garnish each with 2 tablespoons of parsley and 1 tablespoon of Parmesan.

Seafood Chowder

Thaw completely. Bring soup to a boil in a large pot. Add the crab and shrimp, ladle into bowls or cups, garnish with chives and serve immediately.

Three Cheese Spinach Soup

Thaw completely. Heat in a large pot on medium heat. Ladle the soup from pot into six bowls. Garnish with $\frac{1}{4}$ cup Parmesan and serve hot.

Cremini Mushroom and Caramelized Onion Soup

Thaw completely. Heat a large sauté pan on low and simmer soup on stove for 1 hour, stirring often.

Kielbasa Bean Soup

Thaw completely. Slow-cook in crockpot, set on low heat, for 5 to 6 hours. Alternatively, simmer over low heat on stovetop for 2 hours.

Dreamy French Onion Soup

Thaw completely. Ladle soup into six bowls. Float a slice of toasted sourdough bread on top of soup. Place a slice of Gruyère on each bread slice, then sprinkle with 4 teaspoons grated Parmesan and 4 teaspoons grated fontina. Slide bowls under broiler and broil until the cheese is melted, bubbling, and begins to brown. Garnish with chives and thyme.

Seafood Cioppino

Thaw completely. Cook vegetables and broth in crockpot, set on low, for 5 to 6 hours. Add seafood, stir gently, and cook on low heat for 30 minutes more.

Beef and Cabbage Stew

Thaw completely. Ladle into each of six soup bowls and garnish each with 2 tablespoons of parsley and 1 tablespoon of Parmesan.

Seafood Chowder

Thaw completely. Bring soup to a boil in a large pot. Add the crab and shrimp, ladle into bowls or cups, garnish with chives and serve immediately.

Three Cheese Spinach Soup

Thaw completely. Heat in a large pot on medium heat. Ladle the soup from pot into six bowls. Garnish with $\frac{1}{4}$ cup Parmesan and serve hot.

Cremini Mushroom and Caramelized Onion Soup

Thaw completely. Heat a large sauté pan on low and simmer soup on stove for 1 hour, stirring often.

Kielbasa Bean Soup

Thaw completely. Slow-cook in crockpot, set on low heat, for 5 to 6 hours. Alternatively, simmer over low heat on stovetop for 2 hours.

Dreamy French Onion Soup

Thaw completely. Ladle soup into six bowls. Float a slice of toasted sourdough bread on top of soup. Place a slice of Gruyère on each bread slice, then sprinkle with 4 teaspoons grated Parmesan and 4 teaspoons grated fontina. Slide bowls under broiler and broil until the cheese is melted, bubbling, and begins to brown. Garnish with chives and thyme.

Seafood Cioppino

Thaw completely. Cook vegetables and broth in crockpot, set on low, for 5 to 6 hours. Add seafood, stir gently, and cook on low heat for 30 minutes more.

Beef and Cabbage Stew

Thaw completely. Ladle into each of six soup bowls and garnish each with 2 tablespoons of parsley and 1 tablespoon of Parmesan.

Seafood Chowder

Thaw completely. Bring soup to a boil in a large pot. Add the crab and shrimp, ladle into bowls or cups, garnish with chives and serve immediately.

Three Cheese Spinach Soup

Thaw completely. Heat in a large pot on medium heat. Ladle the soup from pot into six bowls. Garnish with $\frac{1}{4}$ cup Parmesan and serve hot.

Five-Spice Grilled Chicken

Thaw completely. Heat a grill to medium-high or a nonstick skillet sprayed with cooking spray. Brown chicken breasts 3 minutes on each side. Reduce heat to medium and cook for 5 to 8 minutes per side.

Parmesan Green Beans

Thaw completely. Heat a large skillet over medium high heat. Add seasoned vegetable mixture and sauté until fragrant, about 5 minutes. Add green beans and ½ cup of water and simmer until beans are bright green and tender, about 8 minutes. Transfer to a platter and sprinkle with ¼ cup Parmesan; serve.

Lemon Rice Pilaf

Thaw completely. Preheat oven to 350°F. Add ½ cup water or chicken stock. Cover with foil and bake for 20 to 30 minutes, until rice is soft but not mushy.

Cajun Dirty Rice

Thaw completely. Place contents in a sprayed baking dish and cover tightly. Bake in a 350°F oven for 1 hour or until liquid is fully absorbed; rice is hot and fluffy.

Wild Rice Salad

Thaw completely. Transfer to a platter, fluff with a fork and serve. A splash of balsamic vinegar would freshen this salad up perfectly.

Holiday Rice

Thaw completely. Preheat oven to 350°F. Cover with foil and bake for 20 to 30 minutes, until rice is soft but not mushy. Sprinkle with Parmesan and serve.

Green and White Bean Salad

Thaw completely. Toss the cheese mixture in the bowl into the bean mixture in a large bowl. Transfer to a serving tray.

Five-Spice Grilled Chicken

Thaw completely. Heat a grill to medium-high or a nonstick skillet sprayed with cooking spray. Brown chicken breasts 3 minutes on each side. Reduce heat to medium and cook for 5 to 8 minutes per side.

Parmesan Green Beans

Thaw completely. Heat a large skillet over medium high heat. Add seasoned vegetable mixture and sauté until fragrant, about 5 minutes. Add green beans and ½ cup of water and simmer until beans are bright green and tender, about 8 minutes. Transfer to a platter and sprinkle with ¼ cup Parmesan; serve.

Lemon Rice Pilaf

Thaw completely. Preheat oven to 350°F. Add ½ cup water or chicken stock. Cover with foil and bake for 20 to 30 minutes, until rice is soft but not mushy.

Cajun Dirty Rice

Thaw completely. Place contents in a sprayed baking dish and cover tightly. Bake in a 350°F oven for 1 hour or until liquid is fully absorbed; rice is hot and fluffy.

Wild Rice Salad

Thaw completely. Transfer to a platter, fluff with a fork and serve. A splash of balsamic vinegar would freshen this salad up perfectly.

Holiday Rice

Thaw completely. Preheat oven to 350°F. Cover with foil and bake for 20 to 30 minutes, until rice is soft but not mushy. Sprinkle with Parmesan and serve.

Green and White Bean Salad

Thaw completely. Toss the cheese mixture in the bowl into the bean mixture in a large bowl. Transfer to a serving tray.

Five-Spice Grilled Chicken

Thaw completely. Heat a grill to medium-high or a nonstick skillet sprayed with cooking spray. Brown chicken breasts 3 minutes on each side. Reduce heat to medium and cook for 5 to 8 minutes per side.

Parmesan Green Beans

Thaw completely. Heat a large skillet over medium high heat. Add seasoned vegetable mixture and sauté until fragrant, about 5 minutes. Add green beans and ½ cup of water and simmer until beans are bright green and tender, about 8 minutes. Transfer to a platter and sprinkle with ¼ cup Parmesan; serve.

Lemon Rice Pilaf

Thaw completely. Preheat oven to 350°F. Add ½ cup water or chicken stock. Cover with foil and bake for 20 to 30 minutes, until rice is soft but not mushy.

Cajun Dirty Rice

Thaw completely. Place contents in a sprayed baking dish and cover tightly. Bake in a 350°F oven for 1 hour or until liquid is fully absorbed; rice is hot and fluffy.

Wild Rice Salad

Thaw completely. Transfer to a platter, fluff with a fork and serve. A splash of balsamic vinegar would freshen this salad up perfectly.

Holiday Rice

Thaw completely. Preheat oven to 350°F. Cover with foil and bake for 20 to 30 minutes, until rice is soft but not mushy. Sprinkle with Parmesan and serve.

Green and White Bean Salad

Thaw completely. Toss the cheese mixture in the bowl into the bean mixture in a large bowl. Transfer to a serving tray.

Black Bean and Rice Salad

Thaw completely to room temperature, garnish with cilantro, and serve with sour cream.

Black Bean and Rice Salad

Thaw completely to room temperature, garnish with cilantro, and serve with sour cream.

Black Bean and Rice Salad

Thaw completely to room temperature, garnish with cilantro, and serve with sour cream.

Kahlúa Baked Beans

Thaw completely. If time permits, let beans marinate overnight. Preheat oven to 350°F. Cover with foil and bake for 45 to 60 minutes. Uncover and bake for 30 minutes more. Alternatively, slow-cook in a crockpot on low heat for 5 to 6 hours.

Kahlúa Baked Beans

Thaw completely. If time permits, let beans marinate overnight. Preheat oven to 350°F. Cover with foil and bake for 45 to 60 minutes. Uncover and bake for 30 minutes more. Alternatively, slow-cook in a crockpot on low heat for 5 to 6 hours.

Kahlúa Baked Beans

Thaw completely. If time permits, let beans marinate overnight. Preheat oven to 350°F. Cover with foil and bake for 45 to 60 minutes. Uncover and bake for 30 minutes more. Alternatively, slow-cook in a crockpot on low heat for 5 to 6 hours.

Layered Strawberry Gelatin Salad

Serve chilled.

Layered Strawberry Gelatin Salad

Serve chilled.

Layered Strawberry Gelatin Salad

Serve chilled.

Corn Bread Muffins

Bake frozen muffins in a preheated 350°F oven for 35 to 45 minutes or until a toothpick inserted in center of muffin comes out clean and muffins are golden brown.

Corn Bread Muffins

Bake frozen muffins in a preheated 350°F oven for 35 to 45 minutes or until a toothpick inserted in center of muffin comes out clean and muffins are golden brown.

Corn Bread Muffins

Bake frozen muffins in a preheated 350°F oven for 35 to 45 minutes or until a toothpick inserted in center of muffin comes out clean and muffins are golden brown.

Baked Shoestring Potatoes

Thaw completely. Preheat oven to 375°F. Bake, uncovered, for approximately 45 minutes, until cheese is melted and bubbly and potatoes are cooked through.

Baked Shoestring Potatoes

Thaw completely. Preheat oven to 375°F. Bake, uncovered, for approximately 45 minutes, until cheese is melted and bubbly and potatoes are cooked through.

Baked Shoestring Potatoes

Thaw completely. Preheat oven to 375°F. Bake, uncovered, for approximately 45 minutes, until cheese is melted and bubbly and potatoes are cooked through.

Pasta

My Big Dream Greek Pasta

Thaw completely. Preheat oven to 350°F. Cover with foil and bake for 45 minutes. Remove foil and bake for 10 minutes more until topping is golden and cheese is bubbly.

My Big Dream Greek Pasta

Thaw completely. Preheat oven to 350°F. Cover with foil and bake for 45 minutes. Remove foil and bake for 10 minutes more until topping is golden and cheese is bubbly.

My Big Dream Greek Pasta

Thaw completely. Preheat oven to 350°F. Cover with foil and bake for 45 minutes. Remove foil and bake for 10 minutes more until topping is golden and cheese is bubbly.

Baked Pesto Ravioli with Chicken

Thaw completely. Preheat oven to 350°F. Cover dish with foil and bake for 1 hour or until bubbly.

Baked Pesto Ravioli with Chicken

Thaw completely. Preheat oven to 350°F. Cover dish with foil and bake for 1 hour or until bubbly.

Baked Pesto Ravioli with Chicken

Thaw completely. Preheat oven to 350°F. Cover dish with foil and bake for 1 hour or until bubbly.

Fettuccine with Chicken and Asparagus

Thaw completely. Preheat oven to 350°F. Cover baking dish with foil and bake for 45 minutes, or until pasta is tender and surface is bubbly.

Baked Pasta and Lemon Chicken

Thaw completely. Preheat oven to 350°F. Place chicken and pasta mixture into prepared baking dish. Cover with foil and bake for 45 minutes. Alternatively, heat a large sauté pan over medium-high heat. Cook for 15 to 20 minutes, until the chicken is cooked through.

Penne with Rosemary Chicken

Thaw completely. Preheat oven to 350°F. Place all ingredients in prepared baking dish; cover with foil. Bake for 1 to 1¼ hours. Alternatively, place in a crockpot set on low heat and cook for 4 hours.

Summer Pasta

Thaw completely. Transfer chicken and pasta mixture to prepared baking dish. Cover with foil and bake in 350°F degree oven for 20 minutes or until thoroughly heated through and mozzarella is soft and just starting to melt.

Manicotti

Thaw completely. Preheat oven to 350°F. Cover with foil and bake for 45 minutes to 1 hour, until the sauce is bubbly.

Tuna Tortellini Gratin

Thaw completely. Preheat oven to 350°F. Cover with foil and bake for 45 minutes to 1 hour. Remove foil and slide dish under broiler for 3 to 4 minutes or until topping is golden brown.

Fettuccine with Chicken and Asparagus

Thaw completely. Preheat oven to 350°F. Cover baking dish with foil and bake for 45 minutes, or until pasta is tender and surface is bubbly.

Baked Pasta and Lemon Chicken

Thaw completely. Preheat oven to 350°F. Place chicken and pasta mixture into prepared baking dish. Cover with foil and bake for 45 minutes. Alternatively, heat a large sauté pan over medium-high heat. Cook for 15 to 20 minutes, until the chicken is cooked through.

Penne with Rosemary Chicken

Thaw completely. Preheat oven to 350°F. Place all ingredients in prepared baking dish; cover with foil. Bake for 1 to 1¼ hours. Alternatively, place in a crockpot set on low heat and cook for 4 hours.

Summer Pasta

Thaw completely. Transfer chicken and pasta mixture to prepared baking dish. Cover with foil and bake in 350°F degree oven for 20 minutes or until thoroughly heated through and mozzarella is soft and just starting to melt.

Manicotti

Thaw completely. Preheat oven to 350°F. Cover with foil and bake for 45 minutes to 1 hour, until the sauce is bubbly.

Tuna Tortellini Gratin

Thaw completely. Preheat oven to 350°F. Cover with foil and bake for 45 minutes to 1 hour. Remove foil and slide dish under broiler for 3 to 4 minutes or until topping is golden brown.

Fettuccine with Chicken and Asparagus

Thaw completely. Preheat oven to 350°F. Cover baking dish with foil and bake for 45 minutes, or until pasta is tender and surface is bubbly.

Baked Pasta and Lemon Chicken

Thaw completely. Preheat oven to 350°F. Place chicken and pasta mixture into prepared baking dish. Cover with foil and bake for 45 minutes. Alternatively, heat a large sauté pan over medium-high heat. Cook for 15 to 20 minutes, until the chicken is cooked through.

Penne with Rosemary Chicken

Thaw completely. Preheat oven to 350°F. Place all ingredients in prepared baking dish; cover with foil. Bake for 1 to 1¼ hours. Alternatively, place in a crockpot set on low heat and cook for 4 hours.

Summer Pasta

Thaw completely. Transfer chicken and pasta mixture to prepared baking dish. Cover with foil and bake in 350°F degree oven for 20 minutes or until thoroughly heated through and mozzarella is soft and just starting to melt.

Manicotti

Thaw completely. Preheat oven to 350°F. Cover with foil and bake for 45 minutes to 1 hour, until the sauce is bubbly.

Tuna Tortellini Gratin

Thaw completely. Preheat oven to 350°F. Cover with foil and bake for 45 minutes to 1 hour. Remove foil and slide dish under broiler for 3 to 4 minutes or until topping is golden brown.

Dream Macaroni and Cheese

Thaw completely. Bake in a 325°F oven, uncovered for 1 hour or until a knife comes out clean when inserted.

Dream Macaroni and Cheese

Thaw completely. Bake in a 325°F oven, uncovered for 1 hour or until a knife comes out clean when inserted.

Dream Macaroni and Cheese

Thaw completely. Bake in a 325°F oven, uncovered for 1 hour or until a knife comes out clean when inserted.

Baked Ziti

Thaw completely. Preheat oven to 350°F. Cover dish with foil and bake for 45 minutes. Remove foil and bake until browned and bubbly, about 10 minutes more.

Baked Ziti

Thaw completely. Preheat oven to 350°F. Cover dish with foil and bake for 45 minutes. Remove foil and bake until browned and bubbly, about 10 minutes more.

Baked Ziti

Thaw completely. Preheat oven to 350°F. Cover dish with foil and bake for 45 minutes. Remove foil and bake until browned and bubbly, about 10 minutes more.

Tried-and-True Lasagne

Thaw completely. Preheat oven to 375°F. Cover with foil and bake for 20 minutes. Remove foil and bake for 15 minutes more, until cheese is melted.

Tried-and-True Lasagne

Thaw completely. Preheat oven to 375°F. Cover with foil and bake for 20 minutes. Remove foil and bake for 15 minutes more, until cheese is melted.

Tried-and-True Lasagne

Thaw completely. Preheat oven to 375°F. Cover with foil and bake for 20 minutes. Remove foil and bake for 15 minutes more, until cheese is melted.

Baked Spaghetti

Thaw completely. Preheat oven to 350°F. Cover with foil and bake for 1 hour. Remove foil and bake 30 minutes more.

Baked Spaghetti

Thaw completely. Preheat oven to 350°F. Cover with foil and bake for 1 hour. Remove foil and bake 30 minutes more.

Baked Spaghetti

Thaw completely. Preheat oven to 350°F. Cover with foil and bake for 1 hour. Remove foil and bake 30 minutes more.

Dinners

Asian Steak

Thaw completely. Marinate steaks in refrigerator for at least 1 hour. Prepare a grill. Grill steaks for 3 minutes per side. Alternatively, heat a nonstick skillet over high heat. Add steaks and sear for 3 minutes on each side, or until internal temperature reaches 100°F for rare, 130°F for medium rare, or 165°F for well done. Remove steaks from heat. Meanwhile, boil marinade for five minutes and drizzle it over steaks.

Asian Steak

Thaw completely. Marinate steaks in refrigerator for at least 1 hour. Prepare a grill. Grill steaks for 3 minutes per side. Alternatively, heat a nonstick skillet over high heat. Add steaks and sear for 3 minutes on each side, or until internal temperature reaches 100°F for rare, 130°F for medium rare, or 165°F for well done. Remove steaks from heat. Meanwhile, boil marinade for five minutes and drizzle it over steaks.

Asian Steak

Thaw completely. Marinate steaks in refrigerator for at least 1 hour. Prepare a grill. Grill steaks for 3 minutes per side. Alternatively, heat a nonstick skillet over high heat. Add steaks and sear for 3 minutes on each side, or until internal temperature reaches 100°F for rare, 130°F for medium rare, or 165°F for well done. Remove steaks from heat. Meanwhile, boil marinade for five minutes and drizzle it over steaks.

Pepper Steak

Thaw completely. Cook in crockpot for 6 to 8 hours on low setting or until internal temperature of meat reaches 165°F.

Pepper Steak

Thaw completely. Cook in crockpot for 6 to 8 hours on low setting or until internal temperature of meat reaches 165°F.

Pepper Steak

Thaw completely. Cook in crockpot for 6 to 8 hours on low setting or until internal temperature of meat reaches 165°F.

Provençal Flank Steak

Thaw completely. Preheat broiler or prepare a grill. Remove steak from marinade and sear on both sides, about 5 minutes per side. Meanwhile, pour marinade into a pot and bring to a boil over high heat. Slice flank steak into paper-thin slices across the grain. Drizzle marinade over steak and serve.

Slow-Cooked Barbecued Beef

Thaw completely. Cook roast in crockpot for 6 to 8 hours on low setting, or until meat falls apart easily. Shred beef with a fork and serve over hamburger buns or baked potatoes.

Beef Stir-Fry

Thaw completely. Heat a stir-fry pan over high heat. Add meat and marinade mixture and stir-fry just until edges of steak are browned. Add vegetables and stir-fry for 2 more minutes, or until vegetables are tender-crisp. Serve over 3 cups of cooked linguini, rice noodles or cooked rice.

Sesame Marinated London Broil

Thaw completely. Prepare a grill or broiler to medium-high heat. Grill for 10 to 12 minutes per side, depending on thickness. Let meat rest for 5 minutes. Meanwhile, boil remaining marinade for 5 minutes on the stove and serve over the London broil.

Beef and Zucchini Casserole

Thaw completely. Preheat oven to 375°F. Bake uncovered for 1 hour or until the top is golden brown and vegetables are fork tender.

Provençal Flank Steak

Thaw completely. Preheat broiler or prepare a grill. Remove steak from marinade and sear on both sides, about 5 minutes per side. Meanwhile, pour marinade into a pot and bring to a boil over high heat. Slice flank steak into paper-thin slices across the grain. Drizzle marinade over steak and serve.

Slow-Cooked Barbecued Beef

Thaw completely. Cook roast in crockpot for 6 to 8 hours on low setting, or until meat falls apart easily. Shred beef with a fork and serve over hamburger buns or baked potatoes.

Beef Stir-Fry

Thaw completely. Heat a stir-fry pan over high heat. Add meat and marinade mixture and stir-fry just until edges of steak are browned. Add vegetables and stir-fry for 2 more minutes, or until vegetables are tender-crisp. Serve over 3 cups of cooked linguini, rice noodles or cooked rice.

Sesame Marinated London Broil

Thaw completely. Prepare a grill or broiler to medium-high heat. Grill for 10 to 12 minutes per side, depending on thickness. Let meat rest for 5 minutes. Meanwhile, boil remaining marinade for 5 minutes on the stove and serve over the London broil.

Beef and Zucchini Casserole

Thaw completely. Preheat oven to 375°F. Bake uncovered for 1 hour or until the top is golden brown and vegetables are fork tender.

Provençal Flank Steak

Thaw completely. Preheat broiler or prepare a grill. Remove steak from marinade and sear on both sides, about 5 minutes per side. Meanwhile, pour marinade into a pot and bring to a boil over high heat. Slice flank steak into paper-thin slices across the grain. Drizzle marinade over steak and serve.

Slow-Cooked Barbecued Beef

Thaw completely. Cook roast in crockpot for 6 to 8 hours on low setting, or until meat falls apart easily. Shred beef with a fork and serve over hamburger buns or baked potatoes.

Beef Stir-Fry

Thaw completely. Heat a stir-fry pan over high heat. Add meat and marinade mixture and stir-fry just until edges of steak are browned. Add vegetables and stir-fry for 2 more minutes, or until vegetables are tender-crisp. Serve over 3 cups of cooked linguini, rice noodles or cooked rice.

Sesame Marinated London Broil

Thaw completely. Prepare a grill or broiler to medium-high heat. Grill for 10 to 12 minutes per side, depending on thickness. Let meat rest for 5 minutes. Meanwhile, boil remaining marinade for 5 minutes on the stove and serve over the London broil.

Beef and Zucchini Casserole

Thaw completely. Preheat oven to 375°F. Bake uncovered for 1 hour or until the top is golden brown and vegetables are fork tender.

Citrus Marinated Beef Sirloin Steaks

Thaw completely. Prepare a grill or broiler to medium-high heat. Broil for 5 minutes per side, depending on thickness. Let meat rest for 5 minutes. Meanwhile, boil remaining marinade for 5 minutes on the stove and serve over the steaks.

Citrus Marinated Beef Sirloin Steaks

Thaw completely. Prepare a grill or broiler to medium-high heat. Broil for 5 minutes per side, depending on thickness. Let meat rest for 5 minutes. Meanwhile, boil remaining marinade for 5 minutes on the stove and serve over the steaks.

Citrus Marinated Beef Sirloin Steaks

Thaw completely. Prepare a grill or broiler to medium-high heat. Broil for 5 minutes per side, depending on thickness. Let meat rest for 5 minutes. Meanwhile, boil remaining marinade for 5 minutes on the stove and serve over the steaks.

Sloppy Joes

Thaw completely. Preheat oven to 375°F. Bake pie for approximately 45 minutes or until cheese is melted and bubbly and internal temperature reaches 165°F.

Sloppy Joes

Thaw completely. Preheat oven to 375°F. Bake pie for approximately 45 minutes or until cheese is melted and bubbly and internal temperature reaches 165°F.

Sloppy Joes

Thaw completely. Preheat oven to 375°F. Bake pie for approximately 45 minutes or until cheese is melted and bubbly and internal temperature reaches 165°F.

Beef and Corn Enchiladas

Thaw completely. Preheat oven to 350°F. Cover with foil and bake for 45 minutes. Remove foil cover and bake for 15 minutes more or until cheese is melted and bubbly.

Beef and Corn Enchiladas

Thaw completely. Preheat oven to 350°F. Cover with foil and bake for 45 minutes. Remove foil cover and bake for 15 minutes more or until cheese is melted and bubbly.

Beef and Corn Enchiladas

Thaw completely. Preheat oven to 350°F. Cover with foil and bake for 45 minutes. Remove foil cover and bake for 15 minutes more or until cheese is melted and bubbly.

Summertime Barbecue Spareribs

Thaw completely. Prepare a grill to medium-low heat. Grill meat on low for 1 to 1½ hours, turning every 10 minutes. Bring sauce to a boil and hold at simmer while basting the ribs at each turn.

Summertime Barbecue Spareribs

Thaw completely. Prepare a grill to medium-low heat. Grill meat on low for 1 to 1½ hours, turning every 10 minutes. Bring sauce to a boil and hold at simmer while basting the ribs at each turn.

Summertime Barbecue Spareribs

Thaw completely. Prepare a grill to medium-low heat. Grill meat on low for 1 to 1½ hours, turning every 10 minutes. Bring sauce to a boil and hold at simmer while basting the ribs at each turn.

Shepherd's Pie

Thaw completely. Preheat oven to 350°F. Bake, uncovered, for 1 to 1½ hours or until potato crust is golden brown and vegetables are fork tender.

Shepherd's Pie

Thaw completely. Preheat oven to 350°F. Bake, uncovered, for 1 to 1½ hours or until potato crust is golden brown and vegetables are fork tender.

Shepherd's Pie

Thaw completely. Preheat oven to 350°F. Bake, uncovered, for 1 to 1½ hours or until potato crust is golden brown and vegetables are fork tender.

New England Pot Roast

Thaw completely. Preheat oven to 325°F. Cover roasting pan with foil and bake for 2 to 3 hours, or slow-cook in crockpot on low heat for 6 to 8 hours, or until meat breaks apart easily with a fork.

New England Pot Roast

Thaw completely. Preheat oven to 325°F. Cover roasting pan with foil and bake for 2 to 3 hours, or slow-cook in crockpot on low heat for 6 to 8 hours, or until meat breaks apart easily with a fork.

New England Pot Roast

Thaw completely. Preheat oven to 325°F. Cover roasting pan with foil and bake for 2 to 3 hours, or slow-cook in crockpot on low heat for 6 to 8 hours, or until meat breaks apart easily with a fork.

Reuben Casserole

Thaw completely. Preheat oven to 350°F. Cover with foil and bake for 1 hour. Remove foil and bake for 30 minutes, until browned and bubbly and layers are heated through.

Caribbean Blackened Turkey

Thaw completely. Prepare a grill to medium heat. Remove turkey from bag, reserving marinade, and grill for 5 minutes per side, depending on thickness. Alternatively, heat an oven broiler to high and spray a broiler pan with cooking spray. Place turkey on the sprayed pan and broil for 5 minutes per side, depending on thickness. Meanwhile, boil the remaining marinade for 5 minutes on the stovetop and serve over the turkey tenderloin slices.

Caribbean Pork over Rice

Thaw completely. Heat a skillet over medium-high heat. Add meat mixture and bring liquid to a boil. Pork should be heated through. Serve over rice, garnished with sliced almonds.

Pork Tenderloin with Pears

Thaw completely. If using a baking dish, preheat oven to 325°F. Cover with foil and bake for 2 hours until internal temperature of pork reads 160 degrees on a meat thermometer. Alternatively, slow-cook in crockpot for 5 to 6 hours on low heat.

Cider-Braised Pork Loin Chops

Thaw completely. Heat a large skillet over high heat. Spoon 2 to 3 teaspoons of liquid mixture into pan, then add pork loin slices. Cook 2 to 3 minutes per side. Reduce heat to medium and add remaining mixture, stirring gently to combine. Cover and cook for 30 to 45 minutes and serve.

Reuben Casserole

Thaw completely. Preheat oven to 350°F. Cover with foil and bake for 1 hour. Remove foil and bake for 30 minutes, until browned and bubbly and layers are heated through.

Caribbean Blackened Turkey

Thaw completely. Prepare a grill to medium heat. Remove turkey from bag, reserving marinade, and grill for 5 minutes per side, depending on thickness. Alternatively, heat an oven broiler to high and spray a broiler pan with cooking spray. Place turkey on the sprayed pan and broil for 5 minutes per side, depending on thickness. Meanwhile, boil the remaining marinade for 5 minutes on the stovetop and serve over the turkey tenderloin slices.

Caribbean Pork over Rice

Thaw completely. Heat a skillet over medium-high heat. Add meat mixture and bring liquid to a boil. Pork should be heated through. Serve over rice, garnished with sliced almonds.

Pork Tenderloin with Pears

Thaw completely. If using a baking dish, preheat oven to 325°F. Cover with foil and bake for 2 hours until internal temperature of pork reads 160 degrees on a meat thermometer. Alternatively, slow-cook in crockpot for 5 to 6 hours on low heat.

Cider-Braised Pork Loin Chops

Thaw completely. Heat a large skillet over high heat. Spoon 2 to 3 teaspoons of liquid mixture into pan, then add pork loin slices. Cook 2 to 3 minutes per side. Reduce heat to medium and add remaining mixture, stirring gently to combine. Cover and cook for 30 to 45 minutes and serve.

Reuben Casserole

Thaw completely. Preheat oven to 350°F. Cover with foil and bake for 1 hour. Remove foil and bake for 30 minutes, until browned and bubbly and layers are heated through.

Caribbean Blackened Turkey

Thaw completely. Prepare a grill to medium heat. Remove turkey from bag, reserving marinade, and grill for 5 minutes per side, depending on thickness. Alternatively, heat an oven broiler to high and spray a broiler pan with cooking spray. Place turkey on the sprayed pan and broil for 5 minutes per side, depending on thickness. Meanwhile, boil the remaining marinade for 5 minutes on the stovetop and serve over the turkey tenderloin slices.

Caribbean Pork over Rice

Thaw completely. Heat a skillet over medium-high heat. Add meat mixture and bring liquid to a boil. Pork should be heated through. Serve over rice, garnished with sliced almonds.

Pork Tenderloin with Pears

Thaw completely. If using a baking dish, preheat oven to 325°F. Cover with foil and bake for 2 hours until internal temperature of pork reads 160 degrees on a meat thermometer. Alternatively, slow-cook in crockpot for 5 to 6 hours on low heat.

Cider-Braised Pork Loin Chops

Thaw completely. Heat a large skillet over high heat. Spoon 2 to 3 teaspoons of liquid mixture into pan, then add pork loin slices. Cook 2 to 3 minutes per side. Reduce heat to medium and add remaining mixture, stirring gently to combine. Cover and cook for 30 to 45 minutes and serve.

Chicken in Herbed Mustard Sauce

Thaw completely. Heat a skillet over medium-high heat. Add the chicken and marinade. Bring the marinade to a boil and cook the chicken for 5 minutes per side, allowing the sauce to thicken. Serve.

Chicken in Herbed Mustard Sauce

Thaw completely. Heat a skillet over medium-high heat. Add the chicken and marinade. Bring the marinade to a boil and cook the chicken for 5 minutes per side, allowing the sauce to thicken. Serve.

Chicken in Herbed Mustard Sauce

Thaw completely. Heat a skillet over medium-high heat. Add the chicken and marinade. Bring the marinade to a boil and cook the chicken for 5 minutes per side, allowing the sauce to thicken. Serve.

Herb-Tomato Chicken

Thaw completely. Preheat oven to 375°F. Bake, uncovered, for 40 to 50 minutes, until internal temperature of chicken is 165°F.

Herb-Tomato Chicken

Thaw completely. Preheat oven to 375°F. Bake, uncovered, for 40 to 50 minutes, until internal temperature of chicken is 165°F.

Herb-Tomato Chicken

Thaw completely. Preheat oven to 375°F. Bake, uncovered, for 40 to 50 minutes, until internal temperature of chicken is 165°F.

Swiss Chicken

Thaw completely. Preheat oven to 350°F. Bake, uncovered, for 1 hour or until internal temperature of chicken reaches 165°F.

Swiss Chicken

Thaw completely. Preheat oven to 350°F. Bake, uncovered, for 1 hour or until internal temperature of chicken reaches 165°F.

Swiss Chicken

Thaw completely. Preheat oven to 350°F. Bake, uncovered, for 1 hour or until internal temperature of chicken reaches 165°F.

Chicken Cordon Bleu

Thaw completely. Preheat oven to 375°F. Bake, uncovered, for 45 minutes or until internal temperature of chicken reaches 165°F.

Chicken Cordon Bleu

Thaw completely. Preheat oven to 375°F. Bake, uncovered, for 45 minutes or until internal temperature of chicken reaches 165°F.

Chicken Cordon Bleu

Thaw completely. Preheat oven to 375°F. Bake, uncovered, for 45 minutes or until internal temperature of chicken reaches 165°F.

Chicken Parmesan

Thaw completely. Preheat oven to 350°F. Bake, uncovered, for 1 hour or until internal temperature of chicken reaches 165°F.

Chicken Parmesan

Thaw completely. Preheat oven to 350°F. Bake, uncovered, for 1 hour or until internal temperature of chicken reaches 165°F.

Chicken Parmesan

Thaw completely. Preheat oven to 350°F. Bake, uncovered, for 1 hour or until internal temperature of chicken reaches 165°F.

Teriyaki Chicken

Thaw completely. Prepare a grill or broiler, or heat a nonstick pan over high heat. Cook chicken 10 minutes per side, or until internal temperature reaches 165°F. Meanwhile, in a saucepan, boil sauce for 5 minutes. Pour into a gravy boat and serve with chicken.

Teriyaki Chicken

Thaw completely. Prepare a grill or broiler, or heat a nonstick pan over high heat. Cook chicken 10 minutes per side, or until internal temperature reaches 165°F. Meanwhile, in a saucepan, boil sauce for 5 minutes. Pour into a gravy boat and serve with chicken.

Teriyaki Chicken

Thaw completely. Prepare a grill or broiler, or heat a nonstick pan over high heat. Cook chicken 10 minutes per side, or until internal temperature reaches 165°F. Meanwhile, in a saucepan, boil sauce for 5 minutes. Pour into a gravy boat and serve with chicken.

Chicken Stir-Fry

Thaw completely. Heat a large stir-fry pan over high heat. Add chicken and marinade and stir-fry for 5 minutes, just until chicken loses its color. Remove chicken with a slotted spoon and set aside. Add vegetables to the hot pan and stir-fry for 1 minute. Return chicken to pan, stir-fry for 4 to 5 more minutes, and serve.

Spicy Lime Chicken

Thaw completely. Heat a skillet over high heat. Add chicken and marinade to pan; cook chicken 3 minutes on each side. Reduce heat to medium, and cook until internal temperature of chicken is 165°F, 5 to 8 minutes.

Crockpot Jambalaya

Thaw completely. Set crockpot on low and cook for 7 hours.

Mango Curry Chicken

Thaw completely. Spoon chicken mixture into a crockpot. Cook in crockpot on low heat for 4 hours. Alternatively, heat a wok over high heat and stir-fry the mixture for 20 minutes.

Chicken with Red Potatoes

Thaw completely. Preheat oven to 350°F. Cover and bake for 1½ hours, until browned and bubbly.

Crispy Picnic Chicken

Thaw completely. Preheat oven to 350°F. Bake, uncovered, for 1 hour or until the chicken reaches 165°F on a meat thermometer. Serve hot or refrigerate overnight and serve chilled.

Chicken Stir-Fry

Thaw completely. Heat a large stir-fry pan over high heat. Add chicken and marinade and stir-fry for 5 minutes, just until chicken loses its color. Remove chicken with a slotted spoon and set aside. Add vegetables to the hot pan and stir-fry for 1 minute. Return chicken to pan, stir-fry for 4 to 5 more minutes, and serve.

Spicy Lime Chicken

Thaw completely. Heat a skillet over high heat. Add chicken and marinade to pan; cook chicken 3 minutes on each side. Reduce heat to medium, and cook until internal temperature of chicken is 165°F, 5 to 8 minutes.

Crockpot Jambalaya

Thaw completely. Set crockpot on low and cook for 7 hours.

Mango Curry Chicken

Thaw completely. Spoon chicken mixture into a crockpot. Cook in crockpot on low heat for 4 hours. Alternatively, heat a wok over high heat and stir-fry the mixture for 20 minutes.

Chicken with Red Potatoes

Thaw completely. Preheat oven to 350°F. Cover and bake for 1½ hours, until browned and bubbly.

Crispy Picnic Chicken

Thaw completely. Preheat oven to 350°F. Bake, uncovered, for 1 hour or until the chicken reaches 165°F on a meat thermometer. Serve hot or refrigerate overnight and serve chilled.

Chicken Stir-Fry

Thaw completely. Heat a large stir-fry pan over high heat. Add chicken and marinade and stir-fry for 5 minutes, just until chicken loses its color. Remove chicken with a slotted spoon and set aside. Add vegetables to the hot pan and stir-fry for 1 minute. Return chicken to pan, stir-fry for 4 to 5 more minutes, and serve.

Spicy Lime Chicken

Thaw completely. Heat a skillet over high heat. Add chicken and marinade to pan; cook chicken 3 minutes on each side. Reduce heat to medium, and cook until internal temperature of chicken is 165°F, 5 to 8 minutes.

Crockpot Jambalaya

Thaw completely. Set crockpot on low and cook for 7 hours.

Mango Curry Chicken

Thaw completely. Spoon chicken mixture into a crockpot. Cook in crockpot on low heat for 4 hours. Alternatively, heat a wok over high heat and stir-fry the mixture for 20 minutes.

Chicken with Red Potatoes

Thaw completely. Preheat oven to 350°F. Cover and bake for 1½ hours, until browned and bubbly.

Crispy Picnic Chicken

Thaw completely. Preheat oven to 350°F. Bake, uncovered, for 1 hour or until the chicken reaches 165°F on a meat thermometer. Serve hot or refrigerate overnight and serve chilled.

Chicken and Black Bean Chili

Thaw completely. Heat oven to 325°F if using a baking dish for 2 hours. Alternatively, turn crockpot to low and cook for 5 to 6 hours. To cook in stockpot, simmer chili on low heat for 2 to 3 hours, stirring often.

Chicken Potpie

Thaw completely. Preheat oven to 350°F. Cover with aluminum foil and bake for 1½ hours. Remove cover and bake for 10 minutes more until crust is golden.

Chicken and Artichoke Casserole

Thaw completely. Preheat oven to 375°F. Bake, uncovered, for 1 hour or until cheese is melted and bubbly.

Cheesy Chicken and Rice Casserole

Thaw completely. Preheat oven to 350°F. Pour 2 cups of milk into baking dish. Bake, covered, with foil for 1½ hours or until cheese begins to bubble.

Baked Chicken Salad

Thaw completely. Preheat oven to 350°F. Sprinkle top of baking dish with ½ cup almonds and 2 cups Chinese noodles. Bake, uncovered, for 30 to 45 minutes or until top is bubbly and crisp.

Arroz con Pollo

Thaw completely. Preheat oven to 350°F. Bake, uncovered for 45 to 60 minutes or until internal temperature of chicken breasts reaches 165°F.

Stuffed French Bread

Thaw completely. Preheat oven to 400°F or prepare a grill on medium heat. Bake bread in foil for 15 minutes. Unwrap and slice into 2-inch slices.

Chicken and Black Bean Chili

Thaw completely. Heat oven to 325°F if using a baking dish for 2 hours. Alternatively, turn crockpot to low and cook for 5 to 6 hours. To cook in stockpot, simmer chili on low heat for 2 to 3 hours, stirring often.

Chicken Potpie

Thaw completely. Preheat oven to 350°F. Cover with aluminum foil and bake for 1½ hours. Remove cover and bake for 10 minutes more until crust is golden.

Chicken and Artichoke Casserole

Thaw completely. Preheat oven to 375°F. Bake, uncovered, for 1 hour or until cheese is melted and bubbly.

Cheesy Chicken and Rice Casserole

Thaw completely. Preheat oven to 350°F. Pour 2 cups of milk into baking dish. Bake, covered, with foil for 1½ hours or until cheese begins to bubble.

Baked Chicken Salad

Thaw completely. Preheat oven to 350°F. Sprinkle top of baking dish with ½ cup almonds and 2 cups Chinese noodles. Bake, uncovered, for 30 to 45 minutes or until top is bubbly and crisp.

Arroz con Pollo

Thaw completely. Preheat oven to 350°F. Bake, uncovered for 45 to 60 minutes or until internal temperature of chicken breasts reaches 165°F.

Stuffed French Bread

Thaw completely. Preheat oven to 400°F or prepare a grill on medium heat. Bake bread in foil for 15 minutes. Unwrap and slice into 2-inch slices.

Chicken and Black Bean Chili

Thaw completely. Heat oven to 325°F if using a baking dish for 2 hours. Alternatively, turn crockpot to low and cook for 5 to 6 hours. To cook in stockpot, simmer chili on low heat for 2 to 3 hours, stirring often.

Chicken Potpie

Thaw completely. Preheat oven to 350°F. Cover with aluminum foil and bake for 1½ hours. Remove cover and bake for 10 minutes more until crust is golden.

Chicken and Artichoke Casserole

Thaw completely. Preheat oven to 375°F. Bake, uncovered, for 1 hour or until cheese is melted and bubbly.

Cheesy Chicken and Rice Casserole

Thaw completely. Preheat oven to 350°F. Pour 2 cups of milk into baking dish. Bake, covered, with foil for 1½ hours or until cheese begins to bubble.

Baked Chicken Salad

Thaw completely. Preheat oven to 350°F. Sprinkle top of baking dish with ½ cup almonds and 2 cups Chinese noodles. Bake, uncovered, for 30 to 45 minutes or until top is bubbly and crisp.

Arroz con Pollo

Thaw completely. Preheat oven to 350°F. Bake, uncovered for 45 to 60 minutes or until internal temperature of chicken breasts reaches 165°F.

Stuffed French Bread

Thaw completely. Preheat oven to 400°F or prepare a grill on medium heat. Bake bread in foil for 15 minutes. Unwrap and slice into 2-inch slices.

Parmesan-Crusted Fish Fillets

Thaw completely. Preheat oven to 450°F. Bake, uncovered, for 8 to 10 minutes until crisp and golden.

Parmesan-Crusted Fish Fillets

Thaw completely. Preheat oven to 450°F. Bake, uncovered, for 8 to 10 minutes until crisp and golden.

Parmesan-Crusted Fish Fillets

Thaw completely. Preheat oven to 450°F. Bake, uncovered, for 8 to 10 minutes until crisp and golden.

Sake and Soy Marinated Salmon

Thaw completely. Preheat oven to 450°F. Remove salmon from marinade with a slotted spoon. Wrap in foil and roast in oven for 8 to 10 minutes. Alternatively, prepare a grill and cook fillets for about 5 minutes until meat flakes away when poked with a fork. Meanwhile, bring marinade to a full boil in a pan, reduce heat, and simmer until reduced by half. Drizzle sauce over salmon and serve.

Sake and Soy Marinated Salmon

Thaw completely. Preheat oven to 450°F. Remove salmon from marinade with a slotted spoon. Wrap in foil and roast in oven for 8 to 10 minutes. Alternatively, prepare a grill and cook fillets for about 5 minutes until meat flakes away when poked with a fork. Meanwhile, bring marinade to a full boil in a pan, reduce heat, and simmer until reduced by half. Drizzle sauce over salmon and serve.

Sake and Soy Marinated Salmon

Thaw completely. Preheat oven to 450°F. Remove salmon from marinade with a slotted spoon. Wrap in foil and roast in oven for 8 to 10 minutes. Alternatively, prepare a grill and cook fillets for about 5 minutes until meat flakes away when poked with a fork. Meanwhile, bring marinade to a full boil in a pan, reduce heat, and simmer until reduced by half. Drizzle sauce over salmon and serve.

Roasted Mediterranean Halibut

Thaw completely. Preheat oven to 450°F. Roast halibut, uncovered, for 10 minutes or until a thin bladed knife passes through center with ease.

Roasted Mediterranean Halibut

Thaw completely. Preheat oven to 450°F. Roast halibut, uncovered, for 10 minutes or until a thin bladed knife passes through center with ease.

Roasted Mediterranean Halibut

Thaw completely. Preheat oven to 450°F. Roast halibut, uncovered, for 10 minutes or until a thin bladed knife passes through center with ease.

Dill Shrimp with Angel Hair Pasta

Thaw completely. Cook the pasta in a large pot of boiling water. Heat a skillet over high heat. Add the shrimp mixture and marinade and cook until the shrimp turn pink, about 5 minutes. Place pasta on a large rimmed platter, spoon the shrimp over the top, and serve.

Dill Shrimp with Angel Hair Pasta

Thaw completely. Cook the pasta in a large pot of boiling water. Heat a skillet over high heat. Add the shrimp mixture and marinade and cook until the shrimp turn pink, about 5 minutes. Place pasta on a large rimmed platter, spoon the shrimp over the top, and serve.

Dill Shrimp with Angel Hair Pasta

Thaw completely. Cook the pasta in a large pot of boiling water. Heat a skillet over high heat. Add the shrimp mixture and marinade and cook until the shrimp turn pink, about 5 minutes. Place pasta on a large rimmed platter, spoon the shrimp over the top, and serve.

Shrimp Creole

Thaw completely. Heat a large skillet over medium-high heat until hot, then add shrimp and marinade. Sauté until shrimp turns pink, about 5 minutes. Serve immediately over rice.

Shrimp Creole

Thaw completely. Heat a large skillet over medium-high heat until hot, then add shrimp and marinade. Sauté until shrimp turns pink, about 5 minutes. Serve immediately over rice.

Shrimp Creole

Thaw completely. Heat a large skillet over medium-high heat until hot, then add shrimp and marinade. Sauté until shrimp turns pink, about 5 minutes. Serve immediately over rice.

Greatest Grub Ever Crab Chili

Thaw completely. Heat a skillet over high heat. Cook vegetable mixture for 10 minutes over medium-high heat, stirring often. Add bean mixture and cook for 5 minutes more. Add 2 pounds of crab and simmer for 10 minutes. Serve hot with sour cream.

Greatest Grub Ever Crab Chili

Thaw completely. Heat a skillet over high heat. Cook vegetable mixture for 10 minutes over medium-high heat, stirring often. Add bean mixture and cook for 5 minutes more. Add 2 pounds of crab and simmer for 10 minutes. Serve hot with sour cream.

Greatest Grub Ever Crab Chili

Thaw completely. Heat a skillet over high heat. Cook vegetable mixture for 10 minutes over medium-high heat, stirring often. Add bean mixture and cook for 5 minutes more. Add 2 pounds of crab and simmer for 10 minutes. Serve hot with sour cream.

Vegetable Chili

Thaw completely. Cook chili in crockpot on low heat for 6 to 8 hours. Alternatively, cover and simmer over low heat on stovetop for 2 to 3 hours.

Vegetable Chili

Thaw completely. Cook chili in crockpot on low heat for 6 to 8 hours. Alternatively, cover and simmer over low heat on stovetop for 2 to 3 hours.

Vegetable Chili

Thaw completely. Cook chili in crockpot on low heat for 6 to 8 hours. Alternatively, cover and simmer over low heat on stovetop for 2 to 3 hours.

Vegetarian Tamale Pie

Thaw completely. Preheat oven to 350°F. Bake, uncovered, for 1½ hours or until a toothpick inserted in corn bread topping comes out clean and crust is golden brown.

Vegetarian Tamale Pie

Thaw completely. Preheat oven to 350°F. Bake, uncovered, for 1½ hours or until a toothpick inserted in corn bread topping comes out clean and crust is golden brown.

Vegetarian Tamale Pie

Thaw completely. Preheat oven to 350°F. Bake, uncovered, for 1½ hours or until a toothpick inserted in corn bread topping comes out clean and crust is golden brown.

Desserts

Cinnamon Apple Cake

Thaw completely. Preheat oven to 350°F. Bake for 1½ hours, or until cake is set and topping is golden brown. Serve warm or at room temperature.

Cinnamon Apple Cake

Thaw completely. Preheat oven to 350°F. Bake for 1½ hours, or until cake is set and topping is golden brown. Serve warm or at room temperature.

Cinnamon Apple Cake

Thaw completely. Preheat oven to 350°F. Bake for 1½ hours, or until cake is set and topping is golden brown. Serve warm or at room temperature.

Rhubarb Cobbler

Thaw completely. Preheat oven to 350°F. Bake, uncovered, for 1 hour or until top is golden brown and crisp.

Rhubarb Cobbler

Thaw completely. Preheat oven to 350°F. Bake, uncovered, for 1 hour or until top is golden brown and crisp.

Rhubarb Cobbler

Thaw completely. Preheat oven to 350°F. Bake, uncovered, for 1 hour or until top is golden brown and crisp.

Pumpkin Icebox Pie

Remove pie from freezer 15 minutes before serving and cut into squares.

Pumpkin Icebox Pie

Remove pie from freezer 15 minutes before serving and cut into squares.

Pumpkin Icebox Pie

Remove pie from freezer 15 minutes before serving and cut into squares.

Dreamy Peanut Butter and Chocolate Cream Pie

Serve frozen.

Dreamy Peanut Butter and Chocolate Cream Pie

Serve frozen.

Dreamy Peanut Butter and Chocolate Cream Pie

Serve frozen.

Pecan Pie

Thaw completely. Preheat oven to 350°F. Bake, uncovered, for 30 minutes. Cool completely before cutting into bars.

Pecan Pie

Thaw completely. Preheat oven to 350°F. Bake, uncovered, for 30 minutes. Cool completely before cutting into bars.

Pecan Pie

Thaw completely. Preheat oven to 350°F. Bake, uncovered, for 30 minutes. Cool completely before cutting into bars.

Quick Raspberry Pie

Serve chilled.

Quick Raspberry Pie

Serve chilled.

Quick Raspberry Pie

Serve chilled.

Frozen Mandarin Orange Parfait

Serve frozen, cut into squares.

Fresh Peach Sorbet

Serve frozen.

Grammy's Chocolate Chip Cookies

Preheat oven to 350°F. Spread dough into jelly roll pan and bake for 20 to 30 minutes. Remove from oven when cookie dough is set and cut into bars. Cool and remove bars from pan. Alternatively, preheat oven to 375° F. Scoop 1-inch balls from mix using an ice-cream scoop and arrange on a prepared baking sheet 2 inches apart. Bake for 10 minutes. Remove cookies from sheet while still warm and cool on a rack or waxed paper.

Harvest Bread

Thaw completely. Preheat oven to 350°F. Bake for 65 to 70 minutes or until golden brown and bread springs back when pressed lightly.

The Best Banana Bread

Thaw completely. Preheat oven to 350°F. Bake for 65 to 70 minutes or until golden brown and bread springs back when pressed lightly.

Grandma Rue's Peanut Butter Fingers

Thaw completely. Cut into bars and serve.

Frozen Mandarin Orange Parfait

Serve frozen, cut into squares.

Fresh Peach Sorbet

Serve frozen.

Grammy's Chocolate Chip Cookies

Preheat oven to 350°F. Spread dough into jelly roll pan and bake for 20 to 30 minutes. Remove from oven when cookie dough is set and cut into bars. Cool and remove bars from pan. Alternatively, preheat oven to 375° F. Scoop 1-inch balls from mix using an ice-cream scoop and arrange on a prepared baking sheet 2 inches apart. Bake for 10 minutes. Remove cookies from sheet while still warm and cool on a rack or waxed paper.

Harvest Bread

Thaw completely. Preheat oven to 350°F. Bake for 65 to 70 minutes or until golden brown and bread springs back when pressed lightly.

The Best Banana Bread

Thaw completely. Preheat oven to 350°F. Bake for 65 to 70 minutes or until golden brown and bread springs back when pressed lightly.

Grandma Rue's Peanut Butter Fingers

Thaw completely. Cut into bars and serve.

Frozen Mandarin Orange Parfait

Serve frozen, cut into squares.

Fresh Peach Sorbet

Serve frozen.

Grammy's Chocolate Chip Cookies

Preheat oven to 350°F. Spread dough into jelly roll pan and bake for 20 to 30 minutes. Remove from oven when cookie dough is set and cut into bars. Cool and remove bars from pan. Alternatively, preheat oven to 375° F. Scoop 1-inch balls from mix using an ice-cream scoop and arrange on a prepared baking sheet 2 inches apart. Bake for 10 minutes. Remove cookies from sheet while still warm and cool on a rack or waxed paper.

Harvest Bread

Thaw completely. Preheat oven to 350°F. Bake for 65 to 70 minutes or until golden brown and bread springs back when pressed lightly.

The Best Banana Bread

Thaw completely. Preheat oven to 350°F. Bake for 65 to 70 minutes or until golden brown and bread springs back when pressed lightly.

Grandma Rue's Peanut Butter Fingers

Thaw completely. Cut into bars and serve.

Index

A

B

C

D

E

F

G

H

J

K

L

M

N

O

P

R

S

T

V

W

Z

You now have the tools you need to feed not only your families bodies but also their minds, spirits, and confidences. Dinnertime is virtually the only time a parent can establish open lines of communication between family members. *Dream Dinners* empowers you to do exactly that, three nights a week, around your dinner table.

The end of the story isn't a freezer full of meals, it is a stronger family, filled with laughter, love, and healthier communication. You can do this. You can strengthen your family. . . . Life just got easier!